MW01295802

Jesus Is Lord:
Workbook and Study Notes on the Fundamentals of the Gospel of Christ

by David E. Pratte

Available in print at
www.lighttomypath.net/sales

Jesus Is Lord:
Workbook and Study Notes
on the Fundamentals of the Gospel of Christ

ISBN-13: 978-1497564688
ISBN-10: 1497564689

Printed books, booklets, and tracts available at
www.lighttomypath.net/sales
Free Bible study articles online at
www.gospelway.com/instruct
Free Bible courses online at
www.biblestudylessons.com
Free class books at
www.biblestudylessons.com/classbooks
Free commentaries on Bible books at
www.gospelway.com/instruct/commentary
Contact the author at
www.gospelway.com/instruct/comments

Note carefully: No teaching in any of our materials is
intended or should ever be construed to justify or to in
any way incite or encourage personal vengeance or
physical violence against any person.

"He who glories, let him glory in the Lord"
– 1 Corinthians 1:31

Other Books by the Author

Topical Bible Studies

Growing a Godly Marriage & Raising Godly Children
Why Believe in God, Jesus, and the Bible? (evidences)
The God of the Bible (study of the Father, Son, and Holy Spirit)
Grace, Faith, and Obedience: The Gospel or Calvinism?
Kingdom of Christ: Future Millennium or Present Spiritual Reign?
Do Not Sin Against the Child: Abortion, Unborn Life, & the Bible
True Words of God: Bible Inspiration and Preservation

Commentaries

Commentary on the Book of Genesis
Commentary on the Books of Joshua and Ruth
Commentary on Ezra, Nehemiah, and Esther
Commentary on Job
Commentary on the Gospel of John
Commentary on the Book of Acts
Commentary on the Book of Hebrews

Bible Question Class Books

Genesis	*Acts*
Joshua and Ruth	*Romans*
1 Samuel	*1 Corinthians*
Ezra, Nehemiah, and Esther	*2 Corinthians and Galatians*
Job	*1 & 2 Timothy, Titus, Philemon*
Isaiah	*Hebrews*
Gospel of Mark	*General Epistles (James - Jude)*
Gospel of Luke	*Revelation*
Gospel of John	

Workbooks with Study Notes

Jesus Is Lord: Workbook on the Fundamentals of the Gospel of Christ
Following Jesus: Workbook on Discipleship
God's Eternal Purpose in Christ: Workbook on the Theme of the Bible

Table of Contents

(Due to printer reformatting, the above numbers may be off a page or two.)

Notes to the Reader

Unless otherwise indicated, Bible quotations are from the New King James Version. Often - especially when I do not use quotations marks – I am not quoting any translation but simply paraphrasing the passage in my own words.

To join our mailing list to be informed of new books or special sales, contact the author at www.gospelway.com/comments

Introduction:

This workbook was designed for small group study, personal study, or family study. The class book is suitable for teens and up. The material was especially designed as an introductory study to the basic principles of the gospel. However, it can be useful to any students who seek to examine or review the fundamentals of the gospel.

Benefiting from the material will require the student(s) to read for themselves each passage that the material calls on them to read. In group settings, please be sure that all students turn to the passage and follow in their own Bibles as each passage is read. Students will benefit only to the extent that they see for themselves what God's word actually says.

After each passage has been read, discussion leaders should let the students answer the questions. Then take the time to **discuss** the questions and the correct answers. Make sure the correct answer to each question is understood. Ask additional questions as needed to help students see the correct answers for themselves. Encourage student questions and input. Ask frequently if anyone has a question or comment. From time to time ask, "Does that make sense?" "Do you understand that?"

For multiple-choice questions, the student should write the letter of the correct answer in the blank. For fill-in-the-blank or short answer questions, write the correct word or words in the blank, etc.

Note: Unless otherwise indicated, Bible quotations are from the New King James Version. Often - especially when I do not use quotations marks – I am not quoting any translation but simply paraphrasing the passage in my own words.

Finally, I encourage plain applications of the principles studied. God's word is written so souls may please God and have eternal life. Please study it with the respect and devotion it deserves!

For whatever good this material achieves, to God be the glory.

Why Should You Believe in God, Jesus, and the Bible?

Introduction:

Have you ever wondered whether God exists, whether Jesus really is God's Son, or whether the Bible is really true? If not, you are an unusual person. All people ask these questions at times. The purpose of this study is to examine the evidence for some of the most basic claims of the Bible.

What Claims Does the Bible Make?

1. The Bible claims that God does exist.

>>> **Read HEBREWS 11:6.** <<<

1 To please God, what must we believe? (a) whatever our parents taught us, (b) whatever our preacher says, (c) that God exists and rewards those who diligently seek Him. Answer (**write** the letter of the correct answer in the blank): _____.

"In the beginning God created the heavens and the earth" (Gen. 1:1).

2. The Bible claims to be an infallible revelation of God's will.

>>> **Read 2 TIMOTHY 3:16,17.** <<<

2 Where did the Scriptures come from? (a) they are inspired by God, (b) they express the opinions of men, (c) they are ancient legends of unknown origin. Answer: _____.

"...The things that I write unto you are the commandments of the Lord" (1 Corinthians 14:37). [See Eph. 3:3-5; 2 Pet. 1:21; 1 Thess. 2:13.]

3. The Bible claims that Jesus is God's Son.

>>> **Read JOHN 20:26-31.** <<<

3&4 What did Thomas call Jesus? Answer (write the correct word[s] in each blank): My _____ and my _____.

5&6 What must we believe in order to have eternal life? Answer: Jesus is the _____, the Son of _____.

"...we have heard for ourselves and know that this is indeed the Christ, the Savior of the world" (John 4:42). [See also John 8:24; Luke 19:10; Matt. 16:15-18; 10:37; John 1:1,14.]

Note: these claims do not permit compromise. We cannot say, "The Bible is just a good book," or "Jesus was just a great man." The Bible claims it is God's word, and Jesus claimed to be God in the flesh. If these claims are not true, then Jesus is a liar and the Bible is a fraud!

What Kind of Evidence Will We Study?

God the Father is invisible (1 John 4:12). We cannot perform laboratory experiments to determine if He exists, but this does not mean we must accept "blind faith" without evidence. Jesus claimed to be God in the flesh. His life can be investigated like any other historical fact. Likewise, many other claims of the Bible can be investigated by logical and historical evidence.

In our daily lives, all of us determine our beliefs on the basis of this kind of evidence. For example, a hunter may not see an animal, but from its footprints he knows it exists and he knows much about its nature. In the same way, God has left "footprints on the sands of time."

A judge and jury do not physically observe a crime, yet they reach a verdict about what happened by the testimony of witnesses.

>>> **Read ACTS 14:17.** <<<

7 God did not leave Himself without what? (a) people, (b) witness, (c) time, (d) money. Answer: _____.

Let us call God's "witnesses," and you be the judge. Weigh the testimony honestly, then reach a verdict (Rom. 10:17), but remember that you are not determining the guilt or innocence of someone else. Rather, your verdict will determine your own eternal destiny!

Witness #1: The Existence of the Universe

No one can deny the existence of the universe. The question is: what is the *origin* of the universe?

Only two explanations are available: (1) there is an all-wise, all-powerful God who **created** it; or (2) matter is eternal and, beginning from an original simple life form, all living things developed gradually over millions of years by process of **evolution**. Consider which of these two views best fits the evidence.

Life Comes Only from Life.

>>> Read ACTS 17:24-28. <<<

8 What does this verse say is the origin of life? (a) life on earth has always existed, (b) an unplanned accident of nature produced the first primitive life by spontaneous generation in an ancient swamp, (c) life on earth was created by a living, wise, powerful God. Answer: _____.

One of the most firmly established laws of science is the Law of Biogenesis, which says that life comes only from living things. There is no evidence that dead matter can spontaneously generate life.

The Bible agrees with scientific fact, for it says that life came from the eternal, living Creator (cf. Acts 14:15). However, evolution contradicts scientific proof, since it requires that dead matter sometime spontaneously came to life. Which view best fits the evidence?

Living Things Reproduce after Their Own Kind.

>>> Read GENESIS 1:11,21,24,25. <<<

9 What kind of offspring do living things have? (a) the same kind as the parents, (b) with enough time, entirely different things may evolve, (c) you never know. Answer: _____.

Every year millions of living things reproduce, and the offspring is always the same kind as the parent. This is exactly what the Bible says. The offspring of dogs will be other dogs, not fish, birds, or people!

Evolution, however, teaches that all the present kinds are the offspring of previous different kinds, all the way back to one original life form. But there is no convincing evidence for this. Living things adapt to their environment, but where is the proof that they produce totally **different** kinds of living things (fish to reptile to bird, etc.)?

If evolution was true, there should be many fossils of intermediate "links" between present kinds of living things. However, the "links" are still missing!

The Human Race Is Unique.

>>> **Read GENESIS 1:26-28.** <<<

10 Man is created in whose image? Answer: In the image of _____.

11 Man has dominion over what? (a) fish, (b) birds, (c) animals, (d) earth, (e) all the preceding. Answer: _____.

Simple observation shows that man is far above the animals.

Only man has rational intelligence. What animal uses abstract symbols (letters and numbers) to speak, write, or do mathematical calculations? What animal invents new tools and machines, trains animals, uses fire, or records wisdom to pass on to future generations?

Among animals there are many shades of intelligence. If man evolved from animals, why are there no animals with shades of intelligence right up to ours, instead of so vast a gulf?

Only man creates new beauty to appreciate in the form of music, art, poetry, humor, etc.

Only man has a conscience and sense of religious values. What animal by nature feels a sense of guilt or seeks to find and worship the cause of its existence?

If man evolved from animals, how do we explain these vast differences? If we develop new characteristics according to "survival of the fittest," how does appreciation of art, etc., make us more fit to survive?

The Bible, however, easily explains all these differences. Man shares these characteristics in common, not with the animals, but with God in whose image we were made.

Design Must Come from a Designer.

>>> **Read ROMANS 1:20.** <<<

12 How can we see the power and Deity (Godhead) of God? Answer: We see them by the things God _____.

>>> **Read PSALMS 19:1.** <<<

13 What do the heavens declare? Answer: The heavens declare the _____ of God.

Intelligent beings can recognize the work of another intelligent being.

When an intelligent being designs something to accomplish some purpose, that thing bears the marks of intelligence - it is intelligible. Other intelligent beings can study how it works, etc. Even if we have never met the maker, we know he must exist and we can appreciate the degree of his intelligence.

To confirm this concept to yourself, take this test. Try to name one thing that has these characteristics: (1) It appeals to your intelligence - it "makes sense" as a logical, reasonable way to accomplish some purpose. But, (2) you know it did **not** originate as the effort of some intelligent being - it "just happened" by blind chance. Can you name any such thing? A car? house? bridge?

The universe bears countless marks of being designed by an intelligent Being.

Cameras are designed by intelligent beings, but no camera can match the overall performance of the **human eye**. Where did your eyes come from?

Computers are made by intelligent beings, but the **human brain** can surpass computers in many ways. Where did your brain come from?

Factories are made by intelligent beings to manufacture a product. But who made the **human reproductive system**?

>>> **Read HEBREWS 3:4.** <<<

14 As a house must have a maker, who ultimately built all things? Answer: The ultimate maker of all things is _____.

When you consider all the organs of the human body, then all the other plants and animals, the heavenly bodies, and all the complex laws of nature, is it reasonable to argue that all this came without intelligent planning?

Science is founded on the conviction that the universe is **intelligible** - it is so orderly and systematic that the human intelligence is able to grasp much about its working. Doesn't this, of itself, prove that an intelligent Being invented it? And doesn't the fact that much of its working is beyond our ability to understand and to duplicate, prove that the intelligent Being who made it is far superior to us?

Every effect must have an adequate cause! Evolution says that life began by **blind chance** and then random mutations produced all advanced life forms. The Bible, however, says that the all-wise, all-powerful, living God intentionally planned and created the universe and all the life forms in it. As you reach your verdict, you must determine which view is more reasonable and best fits the evidence.

15 Every effect must have an adequate what? Answer: _____.

For more information about evolution vs. creation, see our web site at www.gospelway.com/instruct/instruct.

Witness #2: The Accuracy of the Bible

Although the Bible is a textbook on religion, it often touches on other subjects such as history, geography, or science. It was written 2000-3500 years ago, when scientific error abounded. Skeptics have searched it mercilessly to disprove it. But if, despite this, we find that it contains none of the common errors of its day - if it actually speaks truths that were unknown to scientists till centuries later - then this should strengthen our confidence that it is not from men but from God.

Consider the following examples in which the Bible has been proved to be accurate, even when "scholars" disagreed with it.

History and Geography

The Hittite nation

>>> **Read 2 SAMUEL 11:3.** <<<

16 Uriah was of what nationality? Answer: Uriah was a

_____.

The Bible often mentions Hittites (Gen. 15:19-21; Num. 13:29; Josh. 3:10), but for years skeptics said the Bible was wrong. Then in 1906, Hugo Winckler excavated Hattusa, the Hittite capital. We now know that, at its height, the Hittite civilization rivaled Egypt and Assyria in glory! (See *Biblical World*, pp. 290ff.)

Pithom and Raamses

>>> **Read EXODUS 1:11.** <<<

17&18 Name the two cities the Israelites built in Egypt. Answer: They built _____ and _____.

The Bible says that Israelite slaves built these cities using bricks of clay mixed with straw, then clay and stubble, then clay alone (Exodus 5:10-21). In 1883, Naville examined the ruins of Pithom and found all three types of brick. (See *Biblical World*, pp. 458,459.)

The Book of Acts

Sir William Ramsay was a skeptic who sought to disprove Acts by tracing Paul's journeys. Instead, his studies converted him! The turning point came when he proved that, contrary to accepted views, the Bible was right when it implied Iconium was in a different region from Lystra and Derbe (Acts 14:6). (See *Archaeology and Bible History*, Free, p. 317.)

Consider quotations from prominent archeologists:

"...it may be stated categorically that no archaeological discovery has ever controverted a Biblical reference. Scores of archaeological findings have been made which confirm in clear outline or in exact detail historical statements in the Bible. And, by the same token, proper evaluation of Biblical descriptions has often led to amazing discoveries." - Dr. Nelson Glueck (*Rivers in the Desert*, p. 31)

"...archaeology has confirmed countless passages which have been rejected by critics as unhistorical or contradictory to known facts ... Yet archaeological discoveries have shown that these critical charges ... are wrong and that the Bible is trustworthy in the very statements which have been set aside as untrustworthy ... We do not know of any cases where the Bible has been proved wrong." - Dr. Joseph P. Free (*Archaeology and Bible History*, pp. 1,2,134)

Science

>>> **Read ISAIAH 40:22.** <<<

19 What is the shape of the earth? (a) circle, (b) flat, (c) cylinder. Answer: _____.

Isaiah wrote this when men thought the earth was flat ("circle" = "a circle, sphere" - Gesenius). Today we have pictures taken from space to show the earth's shape, but how did Isaiah know?

>>> **Read JOB 26:7.** <<<

20 How is the earth held up? Answer: The earth hangs on

_____.

Ancient men believed many errors. How did Job know the truth?

>>> **Read PSALM 8:8.** <<<

21 Fish pass through what in the seas? Answer: They swim or pass through the _____ of the seas.

Men knew of no paths in the sea until Matthew Maury read this verse. He searched till he discovered the ocean currents, and became known as the Father of Oceanography. (*Impact*, 9/91, pp. 3,4).

>>> **Read ECCLESIASTES 1:7.** <<<

22 What does this verse tell us about rivers? (a) rivers run to the sea, (b) the sea does not get fuller, (c) rivers go back where they were before, (d) all the preceding. Answer: _____.

Today we understand how this happens by the water cycle and evaporation. How did Solomon know?

The Bible has contradicted unproved theories, but properly understood it has never contradicted any proved scientific fact. Yet it has often stated scientific truths centuries before men knew them.

While the Bible has been repeatedly proved accurate, those who criticize the Bible have been consistently unable to disprove it. This surely strengthens our faith in other Bible teachings.

Witness #3: The Unity of the Bible

The Bible includes 66 books written by 40 different men over 1500 years.

These were men of widely different generations, localities and backgrounds. There were kings, slaves, fisherman, physicians, etc. They lived in Israel, Babylon, Rome, etc., from 1400 BC to 100 AD.

But their writings, when collected, show no contradictions.

Paul does not disagree with Moses, John does not argue with David, etc., though they wrote on the most controversial subjects known to man. Instead, their teachings strengthen and support one another.

Some skeptics claim contradictions exist in the Bible, but ask them to produce one. Most will not even try! Usually they have never really studied the Bible, but are taking someone else's word about it. Proper study can reconcile any supposed contradictions that are suggested.

Mere human wisdom could never achieve such unity.

23 Consider religious teachers who write by **human** wisdom. How often do you find them completely agreeing among themselves? (a) they always agree on everything, (b) they usually agree, (c) complete agreement is rare. Answer: _____.

24 If the 40 Bible writers, having such different backgrounds, do agree completely, what would this indicate? (a) they were not writing by their own wisdom, (b) the Bible must be the product of one supreme Mind, (c) God exists, (d) the Bible is God's word, (e) all the preceding. Answer: _____.

Witness #4: Fulfilled Prophecy

The Purpose of Prophecy

Prophecy proves that the true God exists.

>>> **Read JAMES 4:14.** <<<

25 Can men consistently predict the future? (yes or no) Answer: _____.

>>> **Read ISAIAH 41:21-23; 42:8,9.** <<<

26 What can God do that false gods cannot do? Answer: God can predict the _____.

27 God refused to allow His praise to be given to whom? Answer: _____.

Only a Supreme Being can foretell the future accurately. If the God of the Bible can do this, then He must exist and must be the true God.

Prophecy shows which men were spokesmen for God.

>>> **Read DEUTERONOMY 18:20-22.** <<<

28 If a man tries to predict the future and fails, what can we know? Answer: We can know that what he speaks is not from

_____.

If the Bible writers could infallibly predict the future, surely this would indicate God was working through them. [See also Jer. 28:9.]

Prophecy proves that Jesus was God's Son.

>>> **Read LUKE 24:25-27,44.** <<<

29 What did Jesus say about Old Testament Scriptures? (a) they no longer have any value, (b) He was unable to understand them, (c) they spoke about Him and He fulfilled them, (d) all the preceding. Answer: _____.

Jesus' disciples often quoted Old Testament prophecy to prove that Jesus was the Messiah and that His claims must be true [cf. John 5:39; Acts 2:25-36; 3:18- 26; 10:43; 13:27-39].

Examples of Fulfilled Prophecy

Here are just a few of the hundreds of prophecies Jesus fulfilled:

Subject	Prophecy	Fulfillment
Place of birth: Bethlehem	Micah 5:2	Matthew 2:1-6
Lineage: Seed of David	Jeremiah 23:5	Acts 13:22,23
Virgin Birth	Isaiah 7:14	Matthew 1:18-25
Prophet, priest, and king	Deut. 18:17-19 Psalm 110:1-4	Acts 3:20-23 Hebrews 7:17; 8:1
Fore-runner: John Baptist	Isaiah 40:3,4	Luke 3:2-5
Triumphal entry	Zechariah 9:9	Matthew 21:1-9
Death by crucifixion	Psalm 22:16-18; 34:20	John 19:18-37
Died for others' guilt	Isaiah 53:4-12	1 Peter 2:21-25
Buried in rich man's tomb	Isaiah 53:9	Matthew 27:57-60
Resurrection	Psalm 16:10	Acts 2:24-32

Jesus Is Lord

Though a man might fulfill one or two of these by coincidence, to fulfill all of them would be impossible except by plan of God.

In addition, the Bible often accurately predicted the future of nations and cities such as Israel (Deut. 28:15-64), Tyre (Ezek. 26:3-14), Nineveh (Zeph. 2:13-15), and Babylon (Isa. 13:19-21; Jer. 51:37-58).

Mere men, writing by their own human wisdom, could never have predicted the future like this, but the Bible writers did so time and again. This witness testifies that God exists and that He spoke through these men. Since Jesus fulfilled these prophecies, He must be the Messiah, the King, the Prophet, and Savior God sent into the world.

Witness #5: Miracles

Examples of Miracles

A miracle, according to the Bible, is not just any unusual event, nor would an event be called a miracle just because God caused it. A miracle is an event that is **impossible** by natural law, but is brought to pass by the supernatural power of God. For each passage below, state in the answer blank what miraculous event occurred.

>>> **Read JOHN 11:38-44** (cf. Acts 9:36ff).

30 The miracle was: Jesus raised a man from the _____.

>>> **Read MATTHEW 14:22-33** (cf. 8:23-27).

31&32 The miracle was: Jesus _____ on the _____.

>>> **Read MATTHEW 14:14-21** (cf. 15:32-38).

33 The miracle was: Jesus fed (give a number) _____ men with five loaves and two fish.

Jesus also instantaneously and completely healed all kinds of diseases such as leprosy, blindness, deafness, lameness, withered hands, etc. (John 4:46-54; 5:1-9; 9:1-11,30-38; Acts 3:1-20; 4:22; 14:8-10; 5:12-16; 19:11,12; 9:32-35; Mk. 2:1-12, etc.).

The Purpose of Miracles

>>>**Read JOHN 5:36.** <<<

34 What did Jesus say His works proved? (a) that the Father sent Him, (b) that He was a skilled magician, (c) that God will do miracles today for anyone who loves Him. Answer: _____.

>>>**Read ACTS 14:3.** <<<

35 What purpose was served by the miracles done through Paul? (a) they made Paul wealthy, (b) they proved the Lord spoke through Paul, (c) they proved everybody can do miracles, (d) all the preceding. Answer: _____.

People need a way to distinguish God's true spokesmen from false teachers. This was the purpose of miracles - they "confirmed the word" (Mark 16:20). If men claimed to be directly guided by God and they could do works that could occur only by the power of God, then people would know God was working in those men and they would believe their message (Heb. 2:3,4; Acts 2:22; John 20:30,31; 4:48; 2 Cor. 12:12).

Evidence that Miracles Occurred

Since Jesus and His apostles are not personally in our presence, how can we today reach a verdict whether or not miracles were really performed? We must call the witnesses.

1. The Bible contains testimony from many eyewitnesses to confirm that miracles occurred (John 20:30,31 - note the many examples listed above). Remember that the Bible has been proved to be historically trustworthy.

2. Even the enemies of the gospel testified that Jesus and His apostles did miracles.

>>>**Read ACTS 4:16.**

36 What did the rulers say Peter and John had done? Answer: They had done a great _____.

>>> **Read JOHN 11:47.** <<<

37 What did the rulers say Jesus did? Answer: They said He did many _____.

Whether friend or foe, no one who really saw the works of Jesus and His apostles could deny that miracles were done. Their testimony becomes evidence on which we can base our faith (cf. Matt. 12:22-24; Acts 8:5-13; 13:10-13; Ex. 8:17-19; 1 Kings 18:17-39).

Jesus Is Lord

Miracles are God's stamp of approval on the teaching of Jesus and the Bible writers. This witness testifies that there is a God who possesses supernatural power. Since Bible writers did miracles, they must have been guided by God's power. And since Jesus did miracles, His claims also must be valid: He was the Son of God.

Witness #6: The Resurrection

>>> **Read ROMANS 1:4.** <<<

38&39 The resurrection declared Jesus to be who? Answer: He was declared to be the _____ of _____ by the resurrection from the dead.

The resurrection is God's proof that Jesus is His Son. It is the greatest of all miracles in that, if we accept it, all other Bible miracles are easy to accept. Yet if we reject the resurrection, the other miracles will not matter, since we cannot be saved if we reject the resurrection (cf. Rom. 10:9,10; John 20:28-31).

The Facts Surrounding Jesus' Death

>>>**Read 1 CORINTHIANS 15:3-8.** <<<

40,41,&42 List in historical order three facts Paul preached about Jesus in verses 3,4. Answers: Jesus _____, He was _____, and He _____ on the third day.

43 Verses 5-8 list how many **times** that Jesus appeared to people after His resurrection? Answer: (give a number) _____ **times**. **Note carefully:** The question asks how many **times** Jesus appeared according to the list, not how many people He appeared to.

The four gospel accounts confirm the following facts. Remember that the Bible is historically trustworthy. Virtually everyone concedes these events to be true:

1. Jesus was beaten, nailed to the cross, and pierced by a spear.

2. Roman soldiers examined His body to be sure He was dead.

3. His disciples prepared His body for burial and placed it in the tomb of Joseph of Arimathea.

4. Jews sealed the tomb and placed soldiers to guard it.

5. On the third day afterwards, the body was gone. Many people claimed they had seen Jesus alive again.

7. The disciples began to preach that His resurrection proved He was Christ (Acts 1:3; 2:24-36; 3:15, etc.).

Any explanation offered for these events must account for all the facts. Especially one must explain the **empty tomb** and the **eyewitness testimony of those who claimed to see Jesus alive**. (Note the accounts in Matt. 27 and 28; Mark 15 and 16; Luke 23 and 24; John 18-21; and Acts 1.)

Possible Explanations for the Evidence

1. The theory that the disciples stole the body.

The soldiers were paid to say this (Matt. 28:11-15), but consider:

* This involves men testifying about what happened while they slept! Should we accept this as valid testimony?

* How did the disciples evade the guards who were there to prevent the theft of the body? Note: the punishment for losing a prisoner, especially while sleeping on duty, was death (cf. Acts 12:19; 16:27). If this really had happened, would the soldiers admit it?

* What motive would the disciples have for this? They were persecuted and most died for preaching the resurrection. None gained power, riches, or pleasure. Yet none ever denied his testimony regarding the resurrection. Why do this if they knew it was a lie?

* How would this explain the personal appearances of the body, especially to foes and doubters like Saul of Tarsus (Acts 9) and Thomas (John 20:26ff)?

2. The theory that Jesus did not really die but only "swooned" on the cross and then later recovered in the tomb.

* How can this explain the testimony of the Roman soldiers, the centurion, and the disciples who embalmed Jesus, all of whom said He was dead (John 19:32-34,38-42; Mk. 15:44,45)?

* Jesus had been scourged, crucified, and pierced by a spear. He was three days in the tomb without food, water, or medication. How could He revive, roll away the huge stone, evade the guards, walk the length of Palestine, and still appear healthy enough to convince the skeptical disciples that He was

resurrected? This would be a miracle almost as great as the resurrection!

* Would the character of Jesus allow this? Remember, this would make Him a liar and blasphemer.

3. *The theory that the disciples had "hallucinations" and only imagined they saw Jesus alive after the crucifixion.*

* What happened to the **body**? This theory would mean it would still be in the tomb where the enemies could bring it forth to disprove the claims of a resurrection.

* Were the disciples in a state of mind to hallucinate? People who hallucinate see what they expect to see, but the disciples did not expect to see Jesus alive again. They did not even believe when they did see (Mark 16:11-14; Luke 24:11). Did doubting Thomas and unbelieving Saul hallucinate too?

* How does this explain the number and nature of the appearances? How could so many people have the same hallucination, many of them at the same time? The tone is factual and historical. The witnesses saw, heard, and handled the body (Luke 24:39; John 20:26-29).

None of these theories fit the evidence. The only reasonable verdict is that Jesus presented Himself alive "by many infallible proofs" (Acts 1:3). He truly was raised from the dead. Therefore, He truly is the Divine Son of God, just as He claimed.

Conclusion

The witnesses have now testified, and you must reach your verdict. Remember that the verdict *other* people reach is not nearly so important to you as the verdict *you* reach. **Your eternal destiny depends on your decision.** In order to conclude honestly that God does **not** exist, the Bible is **not** God's word, and Jesus is **not** God's Son, here is what you must do:

1. Explain the existence of the universe without God to create it. What reasonable explanation is there?

2. Disprove the accuracy of the Bible. Skeptics have tried this for centuries without success.

3. Disprove the unity of the Bible. Again, this has been tried repeatedly and unsuccessfully.

4. Explain the fulfilled prophecies. What explanation can there be, other than that the writers were inspired by God?

5. Disprove the miracles. But even Jesus' enemies in the first century could not do this!

6. Disprove the resurrection. What explanation can you give?

What verdict will you reach? ***Do you believe God exists, the Bible is God's word, and Jesus Christ is the divine Son of God?***

Personal application questions:

Do you believe that the hypothesis of evolution agrees with the Bible? _____

What is your reaction to the evidence in the lesson showing the accuracy of the Bible in history, geography, and science? _____

Which view do you believe agrees best with what we observe in nature: evolution or creation? _____

How convincing do you find the evidence we presented regarding the existence of God? _____

If Jesus was not the Son of God as he claimed to be, do you believe He could have fulfilled prophecy and done miracles as the Bible says He did? _____

Can you think of an alternative explanation that would fit the facts following Jesus' death without His being resurrected? _____

State what you believe about the inspiration of the Bible. _____

Resources

The following books were especially helpful in preparing this study and will be helpful to you in further study:

Indestructible Foundations, by Peter Wilson.

Internal Evidences of Christianity, by Homer Hailey.

Introduction to Christian Evidences, by Ferrell Jenkins.

Twilight of Evolution, by Henry M. Morris.

See also *Biblical World*, edited by Charles W. Pfieffer, distributed by Baker Book House, Grand Rapids, MI, 1966.

Is Jesus Really Your Lord?

Introduction:

No one greater than Jesus of Nazareth ever lived on earth.

* Millions of people have claimed Him as their Master.

* All history is measured from the time of His birth.

* He revealed the highest moral standard ever known.

* The Bible, which records His words, has been the best-known and most influential book in civilized countries for nearly 2000 years.

Surely Jesus deserves our careful attention. The purpose of this study is to consider why we ought to honor Jesus as Lord, and what it really means to be His disciple. We begin with some definitions.

"Lord" means a person who has authority over others: a master, chief, or ruler. [Matt. 28:18- 20; Eph. 1:19-23; Luke 6:46]

"Disciple" means a follower, pupil, student, learner: one who adheres to the teachings of the master. [Matt. 10:24,25; 16:24]

Why Should Jesus Be Lord of Your Life?

Why should you follow Jesus rather than someone else?

Jesus Is Our Savior

"He will save His people from their sins" (Matthew 1:21). Sin is disobedience to God's law (1 John 3:4). Note how Jesus saves people.

>>> **Read ROMANS 3:23.** <<<

1 How many people commit sin? Answer: _____ have sinned.

>>> **Read ROMANS 6:23.** <<<

2 What is the consequence of sin? Answer: The wages of sin is _____.

3 Through whom can we receive eternal life? (a) Mohammed, (b) Jesus, (c) our parents, (d) no one. Answer: _____.

All of us ought to be punished eternally, because we have disobeyed God. This punishment is what we need to be saved from. Jesus is our Savior because He can give us eternal life in spite of our sins.

>>> **Read ROMANS 5:6-9.** <<<

4 What did Jesus do to save us? Answer: He _____ for us.

5 What characteristic of God does this demonstrate? Answer: It demonstrates God's _____ for us.

6 When Jesus died, was He dying for **you**? Answer ("Yes" or "no"): _____.

Jesus "bore our sins in His own body on the tree" (1 Peter 2:24). We sinned, so we deserve to be punished, but Jesus, who did not sin, died in our place so we can be forgiven and receive eternal life.

>>> **Read MATTHEW 27:22-35,50-54.** <<<

7 When Jesus suffered, whose sins was He suffering for? (a) His own sins, (b) sins of other people, including you and me. Answer: _____.

"There is no other name under heaven given among men by which we must be saved" (Acts 4:12). No one but Jesus can tell how to receive eternal life. [See also John 3:16; 6:68; 14:6; 4:42; Eph. 1:7].

Jesus Is Lord

Jesus Is the Divine Son of God

The Father said about Jesus, "This is My beloved Son, in whom I am well pleased. Hear Him!" (Matthew 17:5). [Heb. 1:1,2; 2:1ff]

>>> **Read JOHN 20:26-31.** <<<

8 How did Thomas know Jesus had been raised? (a) he saw and touched Him, (b) he just heard about it, (c) he dreamed about it. Answer: _____.

9&10 Whom did Thomas confess Jesus to be? Answer: My _____ and my _____.

11 How can we believe Jesus is Lord and God even though we have not seen Him? (a) by guessing, (b) by examining the evidence in the Bible, (c) by taking a preacher's word for it. Answer: _____.

12 What blessing can we have if we believe? Answer: We can have _____ in His name.

Though Jesus died, He was raised from the dead. His resurrection, along with His other miracles and the prophecies He fulfilled, prove that He is God's Son (Cf. Acts 2:22-36; Rom. 1:4; 1 Cor. 15:1-8). Because He is God's Son, He possesses "all authority in heaven and on earth," so we should obey all His commands (Matthew 28:18-20).

Jesus Will Be Our Judge.

Jesus will someday come again and judge all people.

>>> **Read 2 CORINTHIANS 5:10.** <<<

13 How many people will be judged? Answer: We must _____ appear before the judgment seat.

14 Who will judge us? (a) our priest, (b) Buddha, (c) Jesus. Answer: _____.

15 On what basis will Jesus decide our reward? (a) what our parents did, (b) what Adam did, (c) what we did, (d) all the preceding. Answer: _____.

Jesus' words will judge us in the last day (John 12:48). We need to learn His will and follow it so we can be prepared. [See also Acts 17:30,31; Matt. 25:31-46; Rev. 20:11-15.]

>>> **Read MATTHEW 7:13-15,21-27.** <<<

16 What final destinies face us? (a) either eternal life or eternal destruction, (b) all go to heaven, (c) death is the end of our existence. Answer: _____.

17 How many follow the broad road? Answer: _____ enter the broad way.

18 How many follow the narrow way? Answer: _____ find the narrow way.

19 What must we do to enter the kingdom of heaven? (a) just have faith, (b) call Jesus "Lord," (c) do God's will, (d) just be religious. Answer: _____.

We must hear Jesus in everything He teaches or we will be destroyed (Acts 3:22,23). In religion, as in many areas of life, there are truth and error, right and wrong. For example, 2 + 2 = 4, red light means stop, etc. Other answers to these questions would be error. So in religion Jesus' teachings are truth, and anything different is error. [See also 1 John 4:1,6; 2 Tim. 4:2-4; 2 Cor. 11:13-15; 2 Thess. 1:6-9.]

How Should Jesus' Lordship Affect Your Life?

Many people say Jesus is Lord, yet this does not seem to affect the way they live. Some groups even teach that Jesus will save people if they just believe He is the Savior, even if they do not obey Him. What does it really mean to follow Jesus as Lord? How will it change your outlook on life? Can a person be saved without obeying Jesus?

A Disciple Must Learn and Obey the Lord's Will.

A person cannot possibly earn salvation, yet there are conditions one must meet in order to become and remain Jesus' disciple.

>>> **Read JOHN 8:31,32.** <<<

20 To be Jesus' disciple, what must we do? (a) just believe in Him, (b) just learn His will, (c) learn His will and obey it (abide in it)? Answer: _____.

21 If we know and abide in Jesus' word, what will it do for us? Answer: Make us _____ from sin (see v34).

To be freed from sin, we must obey Jesus from the heart (Romans 6:16-18). Truly a disciple must believe in his master, but the only kind of faith that God rewards is obedient faith (Hebrews 10:39; 11:6-8,30). [See also Gal. 5:6; James 2:14-26; John 12:42,43; etc.]

>>> **Read LUKE 6:46.** <<<

22 Do we respect our Lord if we do not obey Him? Answer: (Yes or no): _____.

23 If we have been practicing some activity that is nowhere taught in the Scriptures, what should we do? (a) quit serving God, (b) find a preacher who justifies the practice, (c) quit participating in it. Answer: _____.

We purify our souls in obeying the truth (1 Peter 1:22-25). Jesus is the "author of eternal salvation to all who obey Him" (Hebrews 5:9). To be forgiven of sins and become a disciple we must: believe in Jesus, repent of sins, confess Christ, and be baptized (Mark 16:15,16; Acts 2:38; 22:16; 17:30; Romans 10:9,10; 6:3,4; etc.) Then we must continue to serve Jesus faithfully throughout life.

[See also Acts 10:34,35; James 1:21-25; Matt. 7:21-27; Rom. 2:5-11.]

A Disciple Must Imitate His Lord.

>>> Read LUKE 6:40. <<<

24 What is the goal of a disciple or servant? Answer: The disciple's goal is to be like his _____.

To be Jesus' disciple, we must deny self and follow Him (Matthew 16:24,25). Often people want forgiveness and the blessings of discipleship, but they do not want to give up their own desires and live according to Jesus' teachings. This is not true discipleship.

>>> Read 1 PETER 2:21-24. <<<

25&26 What did Jesus leave for us? Answer: Jesus left an _____ so we should follow in His _____.

27 How did Jesus live? Answer: Jesus lived without committing _____.

Jesus died so that we should no longer live for ourselves, "but for Him who died" and rose again (2 Corinthians 5:15). Jesus gave His life so we could receive eternal life instead of eternal punishment. The least we can do is to love Him enough to follow His example. In every circumstance we should ask, "What would Jesus do in this situation?" Then do as He would do. [See also Gal. 2:20; 1 Cor. 11:1.]

A Disciple Must Put His Lord's Will First.

Choices in life often consist of setting priorities. What will I do with my time, abilities, money, etc.? For a disciple of Jesus, **top** priority must always be serving Jesus and doing His will.

One who is not willing to make this sacrifice, cannot be Jesus' disciple.

>>> **Read LUKE 14:26-33.** <<< (cf. Matthew 10:34-38).

28 What must a person be willing to give up to be Jesus' disciple (a) loved ones, (b) possessions, (c) his life, (d) all the preceding. Answer: _____.

We should present our bodies "a living sacrifice, holy, acceptable to God ... And do not be conformed to this world, but be transformed by the renewing of your mind..." (Romans 12:1,2). Discipleship is total sacrifice, total transformation of self, total lifetime commitment. Jesus must take precedence over everything else. When we realize what Jesus has done for us, such demands are not unreasonable.

>>> **Read MATTHEW 6:24,33.** <<<

29 How many spiritual masters (lords) can a person serve? Answer: You can have only _____ Master.

30&31 What should be our greatest concern in life? Answer: Seek first the _____ of God and His

_____.

"Therefore, if anyone is in Christ, he is a new creation; old things have passed away; behold, all things have become new" (2 Corinthians 5:17). The decision to become a disciple of Jesus is the most important decision in life. It will profoundly impact your whole outlook and every aspect of your life. Anything less is not true discipleship.

[See also Mark 10:28-30; Rev. 2:10; 1 Cor. 6:19,20; 15:58; 2 Cor. 8:5; Rom. chap. 6; Col. chap. 3; John 15:8.]

For further information about the importance of obedience, see our web site at www.gospelway.com/instruct/instruct.

Could a Disciple of Jesus
Ever Be Lost?

We have learned that a disciple of Jesus must obey Jesus' teaching. But what happens if a disciple ceases to serve Christ and goes back into sin? Some religious people teach that, once a person becomes a child of God, he can never so sin as to be eternally lost. Is this teaching in harmony with the teaching of the Lord Himself and His apostles?

Warnings of the Danger of Falling

>>> Read JOHN 15:1-6. <<<

Disciples are here described as branches "in Christ" (vv 2,5, etc.) who have been cleansed by His word (v3).

32&33 If disciples don't bear fruit and abide in Christ (v2,4-6), what happens to them? Answer: They are picked up and thrown into the _____ and are _____.

(Note that abiding in Jesus and bearing fruit requires obedience - 1 John 3:6,24; John 15:10; Gal. 5:19ff; etc.)

>>> Read 1 CORINTHIANS 9:27 and 10:12. <<<

This letter was written by the apostle Paul to saints in the church (1:1,2). They were striving to gain the imperishable crown (9:25). To do so Paul said he had to bring his body into subjection (v27). Israel is an example to us (10:6,11) showing we should not commit sins (idolatry, fornication, etc. - vv. 7,8).

34 Though Paul was an apostle who had preached to others, what concern did he have? (a) he might be disqualified or rejected, (b) some babies might not be baptized, (c) he might be among the elect. Answer: _____.

35 One who thinks he stands must take heed for what (10:12)? Answer: Take heed lest he _____.

If a person believes he cannot possibly be lost, note that this passage shows that he is one of the very people who are in the greatest danger of falling!

Disciples Who Lost Their Faith

>>> Read HEBREWS 3:12-14. <<<

This is addressed to "holy brethren, partakers of the heavenly calling" (3:1). It describes how Old Testament Israel failed to enter God's rest because they lacked faith and obedience.

36 We too must guard against what? (a) an evil heart of unbelief, (b) departing from God, (c) being hardened through the deceitfulness of sin, (d) all the preceding. Answer: _____.

37 To partake with Christ, what must we do? Answer: We must hold our confidence (faith) steadfast to the _____.

Note: V12 warns that God's people may develop a heart of **unbelief,** like the people of Israel did. Many New Testament examples describe disciples to whom this very thing happened.

Note 2 Tim. 2:16-18; 1 Tim. 1:18-20; 5:8. [See also 1 Tim. 6:9,10,20,21; Psa. 106:12,13,21,24; 1 Tim. 5:11,12; Luke 22:31,32]

38 Can a person please God and be saved eternally if he does not have faith (Hebrews 11:6; Revelation 21:8)? Answer: ("Yes" or "no.") _____.

Faith is essential to salvation. Those who lose it are no better off than those who never had it.

Examples of Disciples Who Fell Away

Simon the Sorcerer

>>> Read ACTS 8:12-24. <<<

Simon believed and was baptized (v13). This is what Jesus said one must do to be saved (Mark 16:16). This is what the other Samaritans did (v12). Simon did **"also"** the same things the others did. If they were saved, he was saved. But Simon later sinned.

39 What was Simon's condition after he sinned again (see vv 20-23)? (a) his heart was not right, (b) he was guilty of wickedness, (c) he was in the gall of bitterness and the bond of iniquity, (d) he would perish if he did not repent and pray, (e) all the preceding. Answer: _____.

The Galatians

>>> Read GALATIANS 5:1-4. <<<

These people were children of God (3:26; cf. 1:2-4; 4:6), who had been set free by Christ (5:1). They had been in grace (5:4). They were in danger of sinning by going back to the Old Testament (5:1) and binding circumcision (5:3,4).

40 What would be their condition if they went back to the Old Testament practice of binding circumcision? (a) Christ would profit them nothing, (b) they would be severed from Christ, (c) they would be fallen from grace, (d) all the preceding. Answer: _____.

Can one receive eternal life if he is severed from Christ (Eph. 1:3-7) and fallen from the grace that saves (Eph. 2:8)?

[See also 2 Peter 1:8-11; 2:20-22; Galatians 6:7-9; Romans 6:12-18; 8:12-17; Hebrews 6:4-8]

This does not mean that serving Christ is impossible. In fact Jesus promises that we can overcome temptation and be victorious (1 Cor. 10:13; Eph. 6:10-18; Phil. 4:13). The point of these verses is to show that being a disciple of Christ is a serious matter. We should not take it lightly. We need to begin serving

Christ, but we also need to continue steadfastly in His work (1 Cor. 15:58; Rom. 2:6,7).

For further information about whether or not a child of God can be lost, see our web site at www.gospelway.com/instruct.

Conclusion

Disciples of Christ have a great reward waiting for them (1 Peter 1:3,4). Serving Christ is not easy, but it will be worth every sacrifice we make (Rom. 8:18; 2 Cor. 4:16-18).

Personal application questions:

Briefly state what you believe about who Jesus is? _____

Do you believe it is possible for a child of God to so sin that he/she will be lost in eternity? _____

How Can We Learn Jesus' Will?

Introduction:

In our last lesson we learned that we should honor Jesus as the Lord of our lives. He is the Son of God who died to save us from our sins, and He will one day return to judge us. We should obey His will, imitate the principles He lived by, and serve Him as our highest priority.

However, Jesus is no longer on earth to personally teach us. Where can we go to learn His will today? This is the theme of this lesson.

Jesus' Teachings Are Recorded in the Bible.

Jesus knew that He would leave earth and return to heaven, so during His lifetime He carefully gave instructions to His apostles. After He left, He sent the Holy Spirit to guide the apostles to write His instructions in the New Testament Scriptures.

>>> **Read JOHN 16:13.** <<<

1&2 What did Jesus say the Spirit of truth would do for the apostles? Answer: The Spirit would _____ them into _____ truth.

> >> **Read JOHN 20:29-31.** <<<

3 How can people believe in Jesus even when they have not seen Him? (a) they can't believe, (b) they need a modern-day prophet, (c) they can believe by reading what the inspired men wrote in the Bible. Answer: _____.

4 What blessing can people receive if they believe what is written? Answer: By believing we can have _____ in His name.

> >> **Read EPHESIANS 3:3-5.** <<<

5 What did Paul do with the knowledge revealed to him? (a) he wrote it down, (b) he kept it a secret, (c) it is still an unknown mystery. Answer: _____.

6 How can other people learn what Paul knew? Answer: We can understand when we _____ what he wrote.

Note that, although the gospel message had been unknown (a mystery) in the past, it was revealed or "made known" to the New Testament apostles and prophets. Now we can know it by reading what they wrote.

> >> **Read 1 CORINTHIANS 14:37.** <<<

7 Whose commands did Paul write? Answer: Paul wrote the commands of the _____.

You and I today can know the teachings of the Lord Jesus by reading **the New Testament Scriptures written by His inspired prophets.**

For more information about the importance of the Bible, see our web site at <u>www.gospelway.com/instruct</u>.

[See also Matt. 10:19f; Luke 10:16; John 14:26; 1 Cor. 2:10-14; 11:23; 15:3; Gal. 1:11,12; 2 Peter 1:12-15,21; 3:1,2; 1 John 1:1-4; 2:1-17; Rev. 1:11.]

The Gospel Is a Perfect Revelation.

Sometimes people wonder how adequately the Scriptures reveal the teachings of Jesus for us today. Do they contain all we need to know, or are there teachings that we need but do not have? Can we understand what is taught? Has the message been lost or perverted over the years, so that we today no longer have the true and complete will of Jesus?

The Scriptures Reveal *All* God's Will for Us.

Remember, Jesus promised that the apostles would receive "all truth" (John 16:13), and they wrote down what they received.

>>> **Read ACTS 20:20,27.** <<<

8 How much of God's will did Paul teach to others? (a) he kept back parts that were needed, (b) he preached the whole counsel of God, (c) there were important truths that he never even received. Answer: _____.

>>> **Read 2 PETER 1:3.** <<<

9 How much of God's will had people in Peter's lifetime received? Answer: They received _____ things pertaining to life and godliness.

>>> **Read 2 TIMOTHY 3:16,17.** <<<

10 For what purposes are the Scriptures profitable? (a) teaching and instructing us in righteousness, (b) reproving and correcting us, (c) completely providing all good works, (d) all the preceding. Answer: _____.

11 If the Scriptures provide us to all good works, then do we need some standard of religious authority in addition to the Bible? (yes or no) Answer: _____.

The gospel is the perfect law of liberty, which is able to save our souls (James 1:21,25). We need no further revelation because the Bible completely reveals all God's will for man. It teaches everything we need to know to be saved. *Since the first-century apostles and prophets received all truth, it follows that any doctrine taught today, which they did not record in the Bible, must not be true.*

[See also Matt. 28:20; Col. 4:12; Heb. 13:20,21.]

The Scriptures Are Understandable.

Remember that the apostles wrote down what had been revealed to them, so that others could understand the message (Ephesians 3:3-5).

>>> **Read MARK 7:14.** <<<

12 What did Jesus expect his hearers to do? Answer: They were supposed to hear and _____.

Notice that Jesus spoke here to the "multitude" of common people and He required "everyone" of them to understand what He taught.

>>> **Read ACTS 17:11.** <<<

13 How did these people determine whether or not the things they heard were true? (a) they searched the Scriptures daily, (b) they needed a college education, (c) they needed a priest to explain it to them. Answer: _____.

Could they do this if the Scriptures are impossible to understand? If people cannot understand the Bible, why did God give it to us?

>>> **Read 1 CORINTHIANS 14:33.** <<<

14 God is not the author (or cause) of what? Answer: _____.

God **is** the author of the Scriptures. Now if the Bible has been written in such a way that it is impossible for men to study and understand it, then God would be the author of confusion. Since He is not the author of confusion, then the Bible must be a book that we can understand.

Remember that the Scriptures are profitable to teach, reprove, instruct, and supply us completely to all good works (2 Timothy 3:15-17). They are able to make one wise to salvation. But if we could not understand the Scriptures, then they would not profit in any of these things.

God revealed the Scriptures so men could understand His will. Anyone who believes God is all-wise and all-powerful, must also believe the Bible is a book that can be understood.

[See also 2 Tim. 2:15; Eph. 5:17; Isa. 55:11; Psalm 119:104,105,130.]

The Scriptures Have Been Accurately Preserved.

The Holy Spirit guided the New Testament writers to record Jesus' teachings so those teachings could guide future generations. In order for the Scriptures to accomplish this, God would have to preserve them.

>>> **Read 2 PETER 1:12-15; 3:1,2.** <<<

15 Peter was writing so that people would have a record of his teachings after he died. What would this message do for them? Answer: It would _____ them of the apostles' commands.

>>> **Read JOHN 12:48.** <<<

16 By what standard will men be judged? (a) by their own consciences, (b) by the teachings of their priests, (c) by Jesus' words. Answer: _____.

Jesus' words will judge men at the last day. This means that Jesus' words must endure till the judgment and must be available to men, so we can know what to do to prepare for the judgment. Jesus' words are preserved for us in the written word of the Scriptures.

>>> Read 1 PETER 1:22-25. <<<

17 What is the seed by which we are born again? Answer: We are born again by the incorruptible seed, which is the _____ of God.

18 How long will God's word endure? (a) forever, (b) 2 generations, (c) like a plant that grows then dies, it was lost in the middle ages. Answer: _____.

>>> Read 2 JOHN 2. <<<

19 How long will the truth be with us? Answer: The truth will be with us _____.

God intended for the faith to be delivered to His people only "once" (Jude 3). He delivered it in the first century, then He preserved it through the centuries till today. We today have the perfect and complete teachings of Jesus in a form we can understand in the Scriptures.

For more information about the preservation of the Bible, see our web site at www.gospelway.com/instruct.

[See also Psa. 12:6,7; Heb. 13:20; Isa. 30:8; 59:20,21; Matt. 24:35.]

Jesus' Instructions for Today Are Found in the New Testament, Not the Old.

Some people believe that we today need a special priesthood or should rest on the seventh day of the week because the Old Testament law required this. Others claim that God never changes His law, so if He ever commanded anything, then everyone must always keep that command. But God once commanded a man to build an ark and another man to sacrifice his son (Gen. 6:13-7:5; 22:1-19). Must we do these today?

God Himself says He has changed His laws about circumcision (cf. Gen. 17:9-14 to 1 Cor. 7:18-20; Gal. 5:1-8; 6:12-16), the Levitical priesthood (cf. Ex. 40:12-16; 29:1-9 to Heb.

7:11-18; 1 Pet. 2:5,9), and animal sacrifices (cf. Num. 15:1-6 to Heb. 10:1-18), just to name a few examples.

These Scriptures clearly prove that God has made changes in his laws. Some commands were intended just for certain specific people, not for all people everywhere. Other commands served a temporary purpose. When they fulfilled their purpose, they were no longer needed, so God removed them.

What about the Old Testament laws, including the laws given through Moses? Are they still in effect today, or do we follow only the teachings of the New Testament?

>>> **Read ROMANS 7:2-6.** <<<

20 When is a woman free from her husband? (a) when she divorces him, (b) when she becomes a Christian, (c) when he dies. Answer: _____.

21 What is our relation to the law? (a) we are subject to it, (b) we are freed from it and joined to Christ, (c) we should still keep parts of it. Answer: _____.

>>> **Read HEBREWS 10:9,10.** <<<

Hebrews is a lengthy comparison of the "first" or "old covenant" compared to the "second" or "new covenant." The first covenant included the animal sacrifices, the Levitical priesthood, the tabernacle, and the "tables of the covenant" or the 10 Commands (see 7:11-14; 9:1-5; 10:1-8). In fact it included "every precept" given through Moses (9:18-21).

22&23 What did Jesus do to these two covenants? Answer: He _____ the first that He may _____ the second.

Because of what Jesus did, "the law" (first covenant) was changed or annulled (7:12,18). It was made old, so it vanished away (8:6-13). All this was done in harmony with God's will, not contrary to it.

>>> **Read COLOSSIANS 2:14,16.** <<<

24&25 What did Christ do to the handwriting of ordinances? Answer: He took it _____ nailing it to His _____.

26 Should we let people judge us for not keeping the Sabbath? (yes or no) Answer: _____.

The Old Testament law, given through Moses, applied only to the nation of Israel and only till Jesus died. The teaching of Jesus for people today is recorded in the New Testament, the gospel. It is the "power of God unto salvation" (Romans 1:16).

For more information about the Old Testament law, see our web site at **www.gospelway.com/instruct**.

We Should Reject Man-Made Doctrines.

Many people today claim to follow Jesus, but they participate in religious practices and organizations that are not authorized in the gospel. Yet the New Testament provides us to **all** good works, so other practices cannot be from Jesus. They are human in origin [cf. Matt. 21:25].

What Does Jesus Think of Man-Made Doctrines?

>>> Read MATTHEW 15:9,13,14. <<<

27 How does Jesus describe our worship if it is based on human doctrine (v9)? (a) it is vain, (b) it is acceptable, (c) it doesn't matter. Answer: _____.

Fallible men cannot know what pleases God without revelation from God. The "way of man is not in himself; It is not in man who walks to direct his own steps" (Jeremiah 10:23). Only by following the teaching of Jesus can we know what is pleasing to God.

>>> Read GALATIANS 1:8,9. <<<

28 What is the condition of one who preaches a different gospel? Answer: He is _____.

"There is a way which seems right to a man, but its end is the way of death" (Proverbs 14:12).

>>> Read 2 JOHN 9. <<<

29 What happens to someone who teaches things not found in the teachings that come from Jesus? Answer: He does not have _____.

Remember that all Jesus' teachings were recorded in the New Testament by the original apostles and prophets. To follow Jesus, we must do **only** the things taught in His word. If we follow practices He has not authorized, then we are following **men** instead of following Jesus.

Even if no passage specifically **forbids** a certain practice, that does not mean the practice is acceptable. Instead, we should ask, "Where did Jesus say we **should** do this?" If a practice is not authorized in His word, we should avoid it.

[See also Rev. 22:18,19; Col. 3:17; Prov. 3:5,6; 2 Cor. 10:12,18.]

Some Examples of Human Authority in Religion

People often accept man-made religious practices without realizing **why** they accept them. Often they are following human authorities such as those we are about to consider. (Note that some of these things do have a right to exist. The danger comes when they are viewed as authority which people follow to determine what they believe or practice.)

Family Religion

Some people think, "It was good enough for my mother (or wife, etc.), so it's good enough for me." This makes the family our authority, instead of Jesus. We should be glad if our families follow the Bible, but most people's families are in error (Matthew 7:13,14). Most Christians in the New Testament had to leave their family religion.

30 If our family is involved in practices not found in the gospel, should we still practice as they do? (yes or no) Answer: _____.

[Note Matt. 10:34-37; Acts 5:29; Gal. 1:13,14.]

Conscience, feelings, sincerity

We need sincerity and a good conscience, but these become the standard for some people. "Just let your conscience be your guide. It doesn't matter what you believe as long as you're sincere."

>>> **Read ACTS 23:1; 26:9.** <<<

31 Even before his conversion, Paul was sincere and had a good conscience. At that time was he (a) right, (b) wrong, (c) it didn't matter? Answer: _____.

One can be sincere and have a good conscience, yet be the chief of sinners (1 Timothy 1:13-15). Your conscience only tells you whether or not you are doing what you believe to be right. Like a clock, it will not be reliable unless it has been set properly.

[See also Prov. 14:12; 28:26; Matt. 7:21-23; 2 Cor. 10:18.]

Preachers

Some people just accept whatever their preacher says. "My preacher is well educated, and he would not mislead me." Preachers can help us learn Jesus' will, but they must not become the standard of authority. Preachers are wrong when they differ from what Jesus said. [See also Acts 17:11; 20:29,30; Matt. 7:15; 15:14; 1 John 4:1,6; 2 Cor. 11:13-15.]

32 Should we accept what our preacher says if he cannot show it in the Bible? (yes or no) Answer: _____.

Church creeds, traditions, and decrees of councils

Many denominations write books that the group follows as authority or doctrinal standards. Any creed that contains more than the Bible contains too much. Any creed that contains less than the Bible contains too little. All human creeds and church laws are made on the assumption that fallible humans can write a better standard than the Bible!

For more information about man-made doctrines and religious confusion, see our web site at www.gospelway.com/instruct.

Conclusion

"And by this we know that we know Him, if we keep His commandments" (1 John 2:3-6). A true disciple devotes his lifetime to serving his Master's will. During your lifetime you must choose whether or not you will serve Jesus. "If you love Me, keep My commandments" (John 14:15; cf. 1 John 5:3). Do you follow Jesus or do you follow men?

Personal application questions:

Do you believe we need any source of religious authority other than the Bible? _____

What conclusion do you believe we should reach about religious doctrines or practices that are not found in the Bible? _____

What do you believe about Old Testament practices that are not included in the New Testament? _____

How Can You Be Sure Jesus Has Forgiven Your Sins?

Introduction:

To receive eternal life according to the gospel of Christ, a person must be forgiven of sins by Jesus' blood (Ephesians 1:7; Matthew 26:28; 1 Peter 2:24). But many people are unsure about whether or not they have been forgiven. Others may think that they have been forgiven, but would be surprised to learn that Jesus does not agree.

Matthew 7:21-23 - Many people, who believe in the Lord, will expect Jesus to accept them at the judgment. Instead He will reject them because they have not done the will of the Father.

Acts 23:1; 26:9 - Saul was a Jew who opposed Jesus in all good conscience, doing what he sincerely believed he should do. Yet he was the chief of sinners (1 Timothy 1:12-15). Clearly he had been misled.

What about you and me? Is it possible we have been misled like these people? Surely this matter deserves our careful investigation.

This study is designed to help you be sure about salvation.

Please begin with a brief self-examination to show where you are now (2 Cor. 13:5). Then we will study what the Bible says about salvation, and you can compare your case to Jesus' teaching.

A Have you made a personal commitment to serve Jesus? (Yes or no) Answer: _____

B1 Have you been baptized? (Yes or no) (If not, skip to question #3.) Answer: _____

B2 If so, about how old were you? Answer: _____

B3 How were you baptized (sprinkling, pouring, or immersion)? Answer: _____

B4 Why were you baptized? (a) to please loved ones, (b) as a sign I had been saved, (c) to receive forgiveness of sins, (d) because others were doing it, (e) to join a denomination, (f) other (write your reason in the blank). (You may give more than one reason.) Answer: _____

B5 After you repented of sin and determined to live for God, about how long was it till you were baptized? Answer: _____

C Suppose a person sincerely does the following things. At what point do you believe his sins would be washed away? When he (a) hears the gospel, (b) believes, (c) repents, (d) confesses Jesus, (e) prays for forgiveness, (f) is baptized, (g) I don't know, (h) other (write in the blank the point at which you think sins are washed away). Answer: _____

The Nature of Sin

Some churches teach that people inherit guilt from Adam through their parents. They conclude that little babies are born guilty of sin. What does Jesus teach? Remember that His teaching is found in the Bible.

Sin Is Committed, Not Inherited.
>>> **Read 1 JOHN 3:4.** <<<

1 What is sin? Sin is: (a) breaking social customs, (b) displeasing other people, (c) violating human tradition, (d) transgression or breaking of God's law (lawlessness). Answer: _____.

2 Sin is something a person: (a) commits (practices), (b) inherits. Answer: _____.
>>> **Read ROMANS 6:16 and John 8:34.** <<<

3 How do people become slaves of sin? (a) they inherit a corrupt nature from Adam, (b) everyone is born a slave of sin, (c) whoever commits sin (presents himself to obey sin) is a slave of sin. Answer: _____.

We may sin in word, deed, or thought, but our own conduct is what makes us sinners.

>>> **Read 1 PETER 2:22.** <<<

4 What sins was Jesus guilty of? (a) He was born a sinner, (b) He was guilty of Adam's sin, (c) He was guilty of no sins because He committed no sins. Answer: _____.

Note that Jesus was a descendant of Adam, born of woman (Luke 3:38; Galatians 4:4). He shared in flesh and blood, being made in **all things** like us (Hebrews 2:14,17). If people inherit Adam's sin, then Jesus must have been guilty of sin. Yet in Him there was no sin, because He **did** no sin (2 Corinthians 5:21; 1 John 3:5; Hebrews 4:15). Therefore guilt is not inherited. People are guilty of sin when they **commit** sin.

>>> **Read EZEKIEL 18:20.** <<<

5 Who bears the guilt of a person's sins? Answer: The wickedness of the wicked will be upon (charged against) _____.

6 What sins are we guilty of? (a) just the ones we commit, (b) our father's, (c) Adam's. Answer: _____.

Sin is doing, practicing, committing things that are not in harmony with God's will. When the Bible says people are "in sin," "slaves of sin," or "under sin," it refers to the guilt and consequences a person experiences because of his own sinful conduct.

We may sometimes suffer in this life because of something our ancestors did (such as a child who suffers because his parent is an alcoholic). But guilt itself cannot be inherited through our parents. None of Adam's descendants bear the guilt of his sin. Adam's sin is upon Adam alone. If you are guilty of sin, it is because of what **you** have done.

[See also Mark 7:20-23; Romans 3:9-18,23; 1 Timothy 6:10; James 1:14,15; 2:10,11.]

Each Person Will Be Judged for His Own Life.

Each person's eternal destiny is determined by his/her own conduct, and it is determined individually. Each person is held accountable for what he did, not for what his ancestors did.

>>> **Read MATTHEW 7:21,23.** <<<

7 Who will enter the kingdom of heaven (v21)? Answer: He who _____ the will of the Father.

8 Jesus will reject those who work (practice/do) what (v23)? Answer: _____.

>>> Read **ROMANS 2:6-10.** <<<

9 To receive eternal life, what must we do (vv 7,10)? Answer: We must continue in _____.

10&11 Who will receive tribulation and anguish (vv 8,9)? Answer: Those who reject (do not obey) the _____ but obey (follow) _____.

Note that, at judgment, **each** will be rewarded according to **his works or deeds** (v6).

>>> Read **2 CORINTHIANS 5:10.** <<<

12 How many people must appear before Jesus' judgment seat? Answer: _____.

13 On what basis will each one be judged? (a) what his parents did, (b) what he has done in the body, (c) what Adam did. Answer: _____.

Note again that the above passages all show that sin is something a person does, works, or practices. Folks who believe in original sin teach that every person is **passive** in becoming a sinner and **passive** in being saved from sin. He is a sinner before he **does** anything and saved without **doing** anything. Jesus' teaching says man is **active** both in sin and in salvation. He becomes a sinner because of what he **does**, and we will see that he must choose to **act** in order to receive God's offer of salvation.

[See also Rom. 1:32; 14:12; Matt. 16:27; Rev. 20:12,13; 22:12.]

Babies Are Innocent, not Guilty.

If original sin is true, then babies are born guilty of sin, totally depraved, destined for eternal punishment. But note what Jesus' word says.

>>> Read **PSALM 106:37,38.** <<<

14 When people sacrificed their babies to idols, what kind of blood did they shed? Answer: They shed _____ blood.

If babies inherited Adam's sin, they would be guilty; but God's word says they are innocent. [Cf. Jer. 19:4,5.]

>>> Read **HEBREWS 12:9.** <<<

15 God is the Father of what? Answer: Our
_____.

Our fleshly nature comes through our earthly fathers (like Adam). But God is the Father of our spirits. He gives the spirit and forms it within man (cf. Zech. 12:1; Ecc. 12:7). If our spirits come from God, not from earthly parents, how can our spirits inherit sin from our parents?

The doctrine of original sin says man is born with a soul that is "wholly defiled." Does the sinless Father in heaven give us spirits that are wholly defiled?

>>> **Read MATTHEW 18:3 and 19:14.** <<<

16 What is taught about little children? (a) they inherit the sin of Adam, (b) we must be converted and become like little children to enter the kingdom of God, (c) they are sinners. Answer: _____.

If little children are guilty of sin and wholly defiled, why should we want to become like them? Does conversion make us like sinners? Does the kingdom consist of those who are wholly defiled?

Jesus considered little children to be acceptable to Him just as they were. He did not require them to be forgiven of sins. Rather, He taught those who are sinners to be converted and become like little children.

No passage of Scripture anywhere teaches that little children are born sinners. Sin is not inherited. God does not hold children accountable for their conduct till they are old enough to understand His will and accept the responsibility to serve Him. Then they become sinners when they themselves participate in sinful conduct. Eventually, we all become guilty and need forgiveness (Romans 3:23).

For more information about inherited guilt and original sin, see our web site at www.gospelway.com/instruct.

Some New Testament Examples of Conversion

People need forgiveness when they themselves commit sin. That forgiveness comes only through Jesus' blood. Jesus died to offer forgiveness to everyone, yet not everyone will receive forgiveness. How can you and I be sure we have been forgiven by Jesus' blood?

The book of Acts contains many examples of people who received forgiveness. Since God is no respecter of persons, we can be saved only if we do as these people did (Acts 10:34; Romans 2:11). Consider a few of these Bible examples. (Note: As you study, please consider the chart at the end of this section.)

The Jews on Pentecost

On a Jewish feast day called Pentecost, Jews came to Jerusalem from all over the Roman Empire. The Holy Spirit empowered the apostles to preach to the people (Acts 2:14-36).

>>> **Read ACTS 2:36-41.** <<<

17 What did Peter tell the people to believe (v36)? (a) Jesus is Lord and Christ, (b) people can save themselves without Jesus, (c) it does not matter what we believe if we are sincere, (d) all the preceding. Answer: _____.

18&19 What did Peter command them to do (v38)? Answer: _____ and be _____.

20 For what purpose were they to do this (v38)? Answer: For the _____ of sins.

Three thousand people heard, believed, repented, and were baptized. As a result, they were forgiven of sins. (See the chart.)

Please note that Peter said these same blessings are available to all people everywhere, as many as hear the gospel, including future generations (v39). This includes you, me, and all people today.

The Ethiopian Treasurer

The treasurer of the queen of Ethiopia had come to Jerusalem to worship. He was returning home riding in his chariot, reading from Isaiah. Then a preacher named Philip approached (Acts 8:26-34).

>>> **Read ACTS 8:35-39.** <<<

21 As Philip taught about Jesus, what did the eunuch want (v36)? (a) baptism, (b) money, (c) a direct revelation from the Holy Spirit. Answer: _____.

22 What did the eunuch have to do first (v37)? (a) pray for forgiveness, (b) tell Philip that he believed in Jesus, (c) pay a fee. Answer: _____.

Jesus Is Lord

The treasurer heard about Jesus, believed in him, confessed his faith, and was baptized. (See the chart.) Would you and I receive the same blessings he received, if we do the same things he did?

Saul of Tarsus

Saul was an unbelieving Jew who was traveling to Damascus to persecute Christians (Acts 8:3; 9:1-3). On the road, Jesus appeared to him.

>>> **Read ACTS 9:3-6,18; 22:16.** <<<

23 What did the Lord tell Saul to do (v6)? (a) wait in the city to be told what he must do, (b) pray through at the mourner's bench, (c) send a financial contribution. Answer: _____.

24&25 What did Ananias tell him he must do (22:16)? Answer: He said to be _____ and wash away his _____.

Saul learned about Jesus, was told what he must do, and was baptized to wash away his sins.

A Summary of Examples of Conversions

People	Hear	Believe	Repent	Confess	Baptized	Result
Jews (Acts 2)	v14-41	(v36)	v38		v38,41	Remission (v38)
Eunuch (Acts 8)	v35	v37		v37	vv 38,39	Rejoicing (v39)
Saul (Acts 9,22)	9:6				9:18 22:16	Sins washed away (22:16)

Have **you** done what these people did?

A Summary of the Steps to Forgiveness

By taking all that God's word says in these examples (Acts 3:22,23), we see that people heard the gospel, believed it, repented of sin, confessed Christ, and were baptized. Notice each of these steps more closely.

Hearing

>>> Read JOHN 6:44,45. <<<

26 What must one do to come to Jesus? (a) see a vision, (b) learn the word of God, (c) pray for a direct message from the Spirit. Answer: _____.

27 Can one be saved without hearing the gospel? (yes or no) Answer: _____.

"You shall know the truth, and the truth shall make you free" - John 8:32.

[See also John 6:63,68; 12:48; Acts 11:14; Romans 10:14-17.]

Faith

>>> Read ROMANS 1:16. <<<

28 What is the power of God to salvation? (a) human wisdom, (b) the gospel, (c) man-made creeds. Answer: _____.

29 Who can be saved by the gospel? (a) all who truly believe, (b) anyone who has a good conscience, (c) anyone who is sincere. Answer: _____.

"Without faith it is impossible to please Him" - Hebrews 11:6. Note that believing alone does not make one a child of God, but only gives him the right to **become** a child of God - John 1:12.

[See also John 8:24; 20:30,31; Romans 5:1,2.]

Repentance

>>> Read ACTS 17:30,31. <<<

30 What does God command men to do? Answer: _____.

31 How many people must do this? (a) some, (b) all, (c) none. Answer: _____.

32 What is repentance (note Matthew 21:28,29)? (a) never committing sin, (b) not getting caught, (c) changing our minds about our sins. Answer: _____.

"God is longsuffering to us-ward, not willing that any should perish, but that all should come to repentance" - 2 Peter 3:9. All people are guilty of sin (Romans 3:23) and must repent to be forgiven. We must change our minds about sin and decide to do God's will always.

[See also Acts 2:38; 3:19; 2 Corinthians 7:10.]

Confession

>>> Read ROMANS 10:9,10. <<<

33 Besides believing, what else must we do to be saved? (a) confess Jesus, (b) believe what our parents did, (c) obey the 10 commands. Answer: _____.

"And Simon Peter answered and said, 'Thou art the Christ, the Son of the living God'" - Matthew 16:16.

[See also Acts 8:37; Matthew 10:32; John 12:42.]

Baptism

Many Scriptures show that all people become guilty of sin because of their own conduct. Bible examples show that, to be forgiven, people must hear the gospel, believe in Jesus, repent of sins, confess Christ, and be baptized for the remission of sins.

The last step in all these examples of conversion was **baptism**. Because this is such a controversial yet important step, our next lesson will look at it more closely.

Personal application questions:

What do you believe about the doctrine that we inherit the guilt of Adam's sin? _____

Have you repented of your sins and determined to live your life according to Jesus' teachings? _____

What Does Jesus Teach About Obedience and Baptism?

Introduction:

In our last lesson we learned that people become guilty of sin when they disobey God's commands. To be forgiven, their sins must be washed away by the blood of Jesus. The teaching of Jesus in the Bible shows that, in order to receive this forgiveness, people must hear the gospel, believe, repent, confess Christ, and be baptized. This lesson continues our study of forgiveness, taking a closer look at obedience, especially baptism.

A Closer Look at Obedience

Many denominations teach that people do not need to obey any commands in order to receive forgiveness. They claim salvation is by "faith alone," so the sinner does not need to do anything to be saved.

Surely it is true that faith is essential to salvation, and that no amount of obedience can **earn or merit** salvation. But what does Jesus' word say about obedience. Can we receive eternal life without it?

Accepting Jesus As Lord And Savior Requires Obedience.

>>> **Read ACTS 10:34,35.** <<<

1 Who is acceptable to God? (a) one who just fears him, (b) one who calls Jesus "Lord," (c) one who fears Him and works righteousness. Answer: _____.

>>> **Read HEBREWS 5:9.** <<<

2 Jesus is author (source) of salvation to whom? Answer: To all who _____ Him.

Jesus is the Savior. But He says He will save those who obey Him.

>>> **Read ROMANS 6:17,18.** <<<

3 To be set free from sin, what must people do? Answer: They must _____ from the heart the doctrine delivered.

Only Jesus can free men from sin. But to be set free we must obey.

>>> **Read 1 PETER 1:22,23.** <<<

4 We purify our souls in doing what? (a) in simply believing in Jesus, (b) in obeying the truth, (c) in praying for forgiveness. Answer: _____.

It is not enough to just recognize Jesus as "Lord." One must *do* the will of the Father - Matthew 7:21-23. Your Lord is whomever you obey (Luke 6:46; Rom. 6:16; Matt. 6:24). If you don't obey, He's not really your Lord (cf. Matthew 7:24-27).

If Jesus is the Savior, then *He* must determine *whom* He will save. If He is the Lord, then we must accept what He says about salvation. He says that, in order to purify our souls, be saved, and enter the kingdom of heaven, we must obey Him, do the Father's will, and work righteousness.

[See also James 1:21-25; Acts 9:6.]

Love for Jesus Requires Obedience.

All people recognize the importance of love. 1 Corinthians 16:22 - If anyone does not love the Lord Jesus Christ, let him be accursed." (Cf. Matt. 22:36-39; 1 Cor. 13:1-3.)

Some people say, "As long as you really *love* God, what you *do* doesn't really matter." But if we don't obey Him, do we really have a proper love for Him?

>>> **Read JOHN 14:15; 1 JOHN 5:3.** <<<

5 If we love Him, what will we do? Answer: We will keep (obey) His _____.

Love must show itself in **actions** - obedience. If we don't obey, we don't really love. So love is essential to salvation, but obedience is essential to love. Therefore, obedience is essential to salvation.

Instead of proving that obedience is not required, the Bible doctrine of love proves just the opposite: obedience **is** required.

[See also 2 John 6; 1 John 3:18; 2:3-6; Rom. 13:8-10; Rev. 2:4,5.]

Faith in Jesus Requires Obedience.

We have already learned that faith is essential to salvation (Heb. 11:6; Mark 16:16; John 8:24 etc.). But some claim we are saved by "faith only," so if we have faith then obedience is unnecessary. Is this true?

>>> **Read GALATIANS 5:6.** <<<

6 What avails in Christ? Answer: What avails is faith _____ through love.

Can faith avail anything if it does not work?

>>> **Read JAMES 2:14-26.** <<<

7 What is the condition of faith without works (v17,20,26)? (a) it is dead (barren), (b) it saves us, (c) it is like the faith of Abraham. Answer: _____.

8 We are justified by works and not by what (v24)? Answer: We are not justified by _____.

Note that the context is discussing whether or not we can be saved by a faith that does not work (v14). Faith is necessary to salvation, but some kinds of faith do not save. Demons believe in God (v19), but they don't obey. Are they saved? Both faith and obedience are necessary.

Bible examples teach us the **kind** of faith we must have to be saved. Notice Hebrews 10:39; 11:8,30, etc. The examples show that people received God's rewards only **after** their faith led them to **obey** His commands. Faith that does not obey is faith that cannot save. Neither faith alone nor obedience alone can please God. (Cf. v7,33,4,17,24f.)

Neither the Bible doctrine of faith nor the Bible doctrine of love proves that we are saved without obedience. Instead, both doctrines prove that obedience is necessary. Faith will not save until it moves us to obey. Obedience is included in justification by faith.

[See also 1 John 3:23; John 6:28,29; Rom. 1:5; 16:26; 2 Thess. 1:11.]

Jesus Is Lord

Repentance Requires Obedience.

We have already learned that repentance is necessary to receive salvation (2 Corinthians 7:10; Acts 17:30; 2:38; Matt. 21:28-32; 2 Peter 3:9). But repentance involves a commitment to quit participating in sin.

>>> **Read ACTS 26:20.** <<<

9 One who has repented should do what? (a) live like before, (b) teach that works do not matter, (c) do works worthy of repentance. Answer: _____.

10 Which of the following must one give up? (a) stealing, (b) homosexuality, (c) drunkenness, (d) an adulterous remarriage, (e) all the preceding. (See also 1 Cor. 6:9-11; Gal. 5:19-21; Matt. 19:9; Luke 3:8-14.) Answer: _____.

For more information about repentance of sexual sins and unscriptural divorces, see our web site at www.gospelway.com/instruct.

Receiving Eternal Life Requires Obedience.

>>> **Read ROMANS 2:5-10.** <<<

11 God will reward each one according to what (v6)? Answer: According to his _____.

12 Eternal life will be given to whom (vv 7,10)? (a) those who continue patiently in well-doing and who work good, (b) those who just believe, (c) those who have godly relatives. Answer: _____.

13 Tribulation and anguish will be given to whom (vv 8,9)? Answer: Those who _____ the truth but work (do) evil.

Should men teach that we are saved without obeying, when the Bible says our eternal destinies will be determined by what we do?

[See also 2 Cor. 5:10; Rev. 20:12,13; 22:12; Matt. 25:31-46; 1 John 2:17; Acts 17:30,31; John 5:28,29; Matt. 16:27; 1 Peter 1:17; Rev. 2:23.]

>>> **Read 2 THESSALONIANS 1:8,9.** <<<

14 Flaming fire and everlasting destruction await whom? (a) those who know not God, (b) those who obey not the gospel, (c) both of these. Answer: _____.

Surely faith is necessary to salvation, but so are hearing the gospel, repentance, love, confession of Christ, and obedience. We are not saved by any one thing alone. All these are required to please God, including obedience. Obedience cannot **earn** salvation, any more than faith or repentance can. But all are necessary conditions in order for God by His grace to be willing to grant forgiveness to any individual.

For more information about the importance of obedience, see our web site at www.gospelway.com/instruct.

A Closer Look at Baptism

In all the examples of conversion that we studied, people were baptized. What does Jesus want us to teach and practice about baptism?

>>> **Read EPHESIANS 4:3-6.** <<<

15 How many true Heavenly Fathers are there? Answer (give a number): _____.

16 How many true baptisms are there? Answer (give a number): _____.

Just as there is only one true God, so there is only one true baptism today. Yet denominations practice many different kinds of baptism. What is the true baptism, and why is it important?

The Proper Purpose of Baptism

Why should a person be baptized? Are sins forgiven before baptism or as a result of it? Some groups say baptism is essential to receive forgiveness. Others say sins are forgiven before baptism, but one should be baptized to join a denomination or as an outward sign he has already been saved. What does the gospel of Christ say?

>>> **Read ACTS 22:16.** <<<

17 When were Saul's sins washed away? (a) on the road to Damascus, (b) before he was baptized, (c) as a result of his baptism. Answer: _____.

18 Note that Saul had previously believed in Jesus and had been praying (9:1-6,11). Most churches would say he was already saved before baptism. But was he? Answer (Yes or No): _____.

One who believes in Jesus must be baptized to wash away sins.

>>> **Read ROMANS 6:3,4.** <<<

19 Into what are we baptized? (a) Jesus and His death, (b) a particular denomination, (c) a social club. Answer: _____.

Jesus Is Lord

20 According to what we have earlier learned, can a person be saved outside Jesus and without His blood? Answer (Yes or No): _____.

21 For each person there must be a point at which he first receives forgiveness. He is in sin before that point, but afterwards, he is forgiven. At what point does this occur? (a) the moment we believe, (b) when we pray for forgiveness, (c) when we are baptized. (See also Galatians 3:27.) Answer: _____.

In Jesus we can find forgiveness (Ephesians 1:7), freedom from condemnation (Romans 8:1), salvation (2 Timothy 2:10), and eternal life (1 John 5:11,12). But to come into Jesus, we must be **baptized**.

Illustration: Before the ceremony, a couple takes several steps toward marriage, but they enter the blessings and privileges of matrimony at the point of the wedding ceremony, not before. So faith, repentance, etc., are essential steps toward salvation; but only at the point of baptism does one contact Jesus' blood.

Note also that, as a result of baptism, we "walk in newness of life" (we are "born again"). We cannot be born again without baptism (see also 1 Peter 1:22,23; 2 Corinthians 5:17; John 3:3,5).

>>> **Read ACTS 2:38.** <<<

22 When does remission of sins come? (a) before one repents and is baptized, (b) as a result of repenting and being baptized. Answer: _____.

23 Can one be saved without repentance? Answer (Yes or No): _____.

24 Can one be saved without baptism? Answer (Yes or No): _____.

As in the Lord's Supper, baptism involves both an outer action and an inner meaning (1 Corinthians 11:23-29). If a person did the outer act but did not understand the inner meaning or did it for the wrong reason, how could his baptism be valid?

>>> **Read MARK 16:15,16.** <<<

25 What must one do to be saved? Answer: He who believes and is _____ will be saved.

26 When is one saved? (a) before baptism, (b) as a result of baptism. Answer: _____.

Just as 1 + 1 = 2, so faith + baptism = salvation. Take away faith or baptism, and you no longer have salvation.

"...Baptism doth also now save us..." - 1 Peter 3:21. The power to forgive is in Jesus' death and resurrection, not in the water. But we receive that power when our faith leads us to be baptized, not before.

For more information about the purpose of baptism, see our web site at www.gospelway.com/instruct.

The Proper Action of Baptism

Does baptism involve sprinkling, pouring, or immersion?

>>> Read ROMANS 6:4 and COLOSSIANS 2:12. <<<

27 How is baptism described? (a) sprinkling, (b) pouring, (c) burial and resurrection, (d) all the preceding. Answer: _____.

When Jesus was buried, was a little dirt sprinkled or poured on Him, or was He was completely surrounded in the earth, then came out from it (compare Matthew 12:40; 27:60)?

>>> Read ACTS 8:38,39. <<<

28 How is the eunuch's baptism described? (a) he was sprinkled, (b) water was poured on him, (c) he went down into the water and came up out of it. Answer: _____.

29 When denominations sprinkle or pour, does the person "go down into" the water and "come up out of it"? Answer (Yes or No): _____.

In the gospel, baptism is always a complete immersion. In fact, the original word meant to dip, immerse, etc. (See the **Greek derivation** of the word according to English dictionaries.)

[See also Mark 1:9,10; Hebrews 10:22; John 3:23.]

For more information about the action of baptism, see our web site at www.gospelway.com/instruct.

The Proper Subject of Baptism

Should babies be baptized, or should people wait until they are old enough to understand the commitment and decide for themselves?

30 Before one can be baptized, he must understand the gospel (John 6:44,45), believe (Mark 16:15,16; Acts 8:12), repent (Acts 2:38), and confess (Romans 10:9,10). Can babies do all these things? Answer (Yes or No): _____.

31 Baptized people are members of the church and must participate in its work and worship (1 Corinthians 12:13,25,26; 10:16,17; 11:23-29; Ephesians 4:16). Can babies do these things? Answer (Yes or No): _____.

In our last lesson we learned that sin is not inherited, and therefore little children are innocent of sin. To enter the kingdom of heaven, sinners must be converted and become like little children. (See Psalm 106:38; Matthew 18:3; 19:14; Ezekiel 18:20; 2 Corinthians 5:10.)

Since baptism is for the remission of sins (Acts 2:38), and since babies have no sin, it follows that they do not need to be baptized. The command to be baptized is addressed to people old enough to make their own choice with understanding. To baptize babies would be to obey the teachings of men, not Jesus (Matthew 15:9; Galatians 1:8,9; etc.).

In the Bible, when people understood, believed, and repented, they were baptized without delay (Acts 2:41; 8:35-39; 22:16; 16:23-34). Many churches today postpone baptism until a "baptismal service" days or weeks later. This shows they misunderstand the purpose of it. If you understand, you should not delay, but obey today.

For more information about infant baptism, see our web site at <u>www.gospelway.com/instruct</u>.

Conclusion

To be sure your sins are forgiven, you must **obey** the teachings of Jesus the Lord, not human doctrines. In our last lesson, you summarized your own relationship to Jesus. Please go back and compare what you have done in the past to what you now know the Bible teaches.

Perhaps you are one of the many people who thought you were forgiven, but now you realize you were misled. What should you do? You should realize that you simply have never completed your obedience to the gospel, and you should now determine to complete it.

In particular, if a person realizes that his "baptism" was not Scriptural, what should he do? Acts 19:1-7 shows that people with this problem needed to be baptized properly. Remember, there are many false baptisms, but only one true baptism (Ephesians 4:3-6).

"Be ye doers of the word, and not hearers only" - James 1:22.

"If you love Me, keep my commandments" - John 14:15.

Personal application questions:

What is your belief about the importance of obedience in salvation? _____

Have you **believed** in Jesus as your Savior who died for your sins, and have you **repented** and determined to dedicate your whole life to serving God? _____

Have you **confessed** Jesus as your Lord and been Scripturally **baptized** - completely immersed, based on your own personal conviction, for the purpose of receiving forgiveness of sins by the blood of Jesus? _____

Jesus Is Lord

Where Can You Find the Church That Belongs to Jesus?

Introduction:

Jesus built His church in the first century (Matthew 16:18). All serious Bible students agree that He built only one church, and all saved people then were in that one church. But today there are hundreds of denominations, differing from one another in name, worship, organization, plan of salvation, etc. Yet all claim to follow Jesus and to please God.

The purpose of this study is to determine what Jesus wants us to practice regarding church membership. What was Jesus' church like in the first century? Does the church that Jesus built still exist today? If so, how can we find it and become members of it? What does God think about all the many different modern churches?

How Important is Jesus' Church?

Why should we study about Jesus' church? Some people think the church has nothing to do with salvation, so people can be saved outside the church. How important is the church to Jesus the Lord?

>>> **Read ACTS 20:28.** <<

1 How did Jesus make the church His? Answer: He purchased the church with His _____.

2 Can we be saved without Jesus' blood? Answer (yes or no): _____.

3 Then can we be saved outside Jesus' church? Answer (yes or no): _____.

Jesus shed His blood to save us from sin (Ephesians 1:7; Revelation 1:5; Romans 5:6-9). But the people who have been saved and purchased by that blood are the people who are in the church!

>>> Read EPHESIANS 5:23,25. <<<

4 For whom is Christ the Savior? (a) the nation of Israel only, (b) the body (church), (c) all people will be saved. Answer: _____.

Salvation can be obtained only through Jesus' death (Acts 4:12; John 14:6; Hebrews 5:9; 7:25). But Jesus died to save the **church**. If the church has nothing to do with our salvation, why did the Lord die for it?

The Lord adds to the church those who should be saved - Acts 2:47. Christ is the Savior, but all those whose sins He has forgiven are in the church. Those outside the church are yet in their sins. This is why it is vitally important for us to learn about Jesus' church. (See also Ephesians 3:10,11; Colossians 1:12-14; Hebrews 10:25; etc.)

For more information about the importance of the church, see our web site at www.gospelway.com/instruct.

The Word "Church" Has Different Meanings.

In the Bible, the "church" always refers to a group of **people**, never to a physical **building**. The word has two primary uses:

1. The church **universally** - the body of all saved people everywhere (Matthew 16:18; Ephesians 5:22-25; Acts 2:47).

2. The church **locally** - a congregation of saved people in a certain area who meet, work, and worship together (Jerusalem, Corinth, etc. - Acts 8:1; 13:1; 1 Corinthians 1:2; Galatians 1:2; Revelation 1:4).

We will study many examples of this word as we proceed.

First let us study the characteristics of the New Testament church, then we will study the origin of the modern denominations.

Part I: What Should Jesus' Church Be Like?

If the police were searching for a missing person, how would they identify the correct person? They would need a **description** or list of identifying characteristics: age, name, height, weight, etc. Likewise, if Jesus' church exists today, how could we identify it?

>>> Read MATTHEW 7:15-21. <<<

5 How can false teachers be identified? (a) by their outward appearance, (b) by their unkind manners, (c) by their fruits. Answer: _____.

6 What are the "fruits" of God's followers? (a) they do the will of the Father, (b) they just call Jesus "Lord," (c) they just believe. Answer: _____.

The true church can be identified because it teaches and practices the will of God. By learning Jesus' will for His church, we can know the identifying marks of His church. Consider these characteristics:

The Doctrinal Standard of the Church

What law or rules should the church follow to determine what it believes, teaches, and practices?

>>> Read EPHESIANS 1:22,23. <<<

7 Who is Head over all things to the church? (a) John the Baptist, (b) Peter, (c) Jesus, (d) Mohammed, (e) a human headquarters. Answer: _____.

8 Whose control, then, should the church submit to? Answer: The control of _____.

>>> Read COLOSSIANS 3:17. <<<

9 What must be done in Jesus' name (by His authority)? Answer: _____ we do, in word or deed.

Since Jesus built and purchased the church, it must follow His directions. Remember, His will is revealed in the New Testament.

(See also Ephesians 5:23; John 12:48; Acts 3:22,23; Matthew 28:18-20; Luke 6:46; Colossians 1:18; 2:19; Hebrews 5:9; 1 Corinthians 14:37.)

May the church follow man-made laws?

>>> Read 2 JOHN 9. <<<

10 What happens if we do not abide in the teachings of Jesus? Answer: We do not have _____.

>>> **Read MATTHEW 15:9.** <<<

11 What does God think of worship that is based on man-made teachings? (a) it is vain, (b) He encourages it, (c) it doesn't matter. Answer: _____.

>>> **Read GALATIANS 1:8,9.** <<<

12 What happens if we preach a different gospel? Answer: We are _____.

13 Would a church be honoring Jesus as Lord if it follows doctrines or practices not found in the Bible? Answer (yes or no): _____.

If Jesus' church exists today, it must strive to listen to all His teachings and must avoid practices not found in His teachings.

(See Revelation 22:18,19; Proverbs 14:12; 3:5,6; Jeremiah 10:23.)

If you would like to learn more about what authority the church should follow, see our web site at www.gospelway.com/instruct.

The Origin or Beginning of the Church

>>> **Read MATTHEW 16:15-18.** <<<

14 What did Jesus promise to build? (a) a social club, (b) an entertainment, recreational club, (c) His church, (d) all the preceding. Answer: _____.

15 Did the church exist when Jesus said this? Answer (yes or no): _____.

16 How many churches did Jesus promise to build? (a) one, (b) ten, (c) hundreds. Answer: _____.

This passage and all passages before Acts 2 speak of the church as coming in the future (see also Isaiah 2:2,3; Daniel 2:44; Mark 1:15; 9:1; Acts 1:4-8).

>>> **Read ACTS 2:47.** <<<

17 Who was adding people to His body (the church)? (Cf. vv 38,41.) Answer: The _____.

Many other passages after Acts 2 speak of the church as being in existence (see Acts 5:11; 8:1-3; 11:22,26; Colossians 1:13; etc.).

So the church that belongs to Jesus began in Jerusalem on Pentecost after Jesus' ascension.

18 Suppose men begin a church at a place and time other than Jerusalem on Pentecost. Would it be Jesus' church? Answer (yes or no): _____.

If Jesus' church exists today, it must be the church that He began on Pentecost in Jerusalem.

The Names or Designations of the Church

Names are important to God. He sometimes named people before they were born, or changed their names later (Genesis 17:5,15,19; 32:27,28; Luke 1:13; Matt. 1:21; Isaiah 62:2; etc.). What terms or phrases does the Lord want people to use to refer to the church and its members?

Terms used for the church:

The **church** of Christ or of God (Matthew 16:18; Romans 16:16; 1 Corinthians 1:2; etc.).

The **house** or family of God (1 Timothy 3:15; Ephesians 2:16,19; Galatians 6:10).

The **kingdom** of Christ (Colossians 1:13; Matthew 16:18,19; Revelation 1:9; Hebrews 12:28).

The **body** of Christ (Ephesians 1:22,23; 4:4-6; Colossians 1:18).

Note that all these terms give honor to God the Father or the Son, and show our relationship to them.

Terms used for individual members of the church:

Disciples (Acts 11:26; 20:7; 8:3; 9:1).

Children of God (2 Corinthians 6:16-18; 1 John 3:2).

Christians (Acts 11:26; 26:28; 1 Peter 4:16).

>>> Read 1 CORINTHIANS 1:10-13. <<<

19 What sin occurred at Corinth? (a) groups were named after men, (b) men were exalted instead of Jesus, (c) division, (d) all the preceding. Answer: _____.

Naming the church after a particular doctrine likewise violates the principles of this passage, promotes division, and fails to exalt God.

One of the fruits of Jesus' church was that it wore names that glorify God and Christ. It never wore names that honored men, were invented by men, or exalted some particular Bible doctrine.

The Steps to Enter the Church

Some churches teach that there are things a person must do to be saved, and then afterward there are other things he must do to join the church. But the church is the body of all saved people (Ephesians 5:23,25; Acts 20:28; Colossians 1:13). Therefore, whenever one receives the forgiveness of his sins, he automatically becomes a member of the church at the same time and by the same steps.

You cannot be voted into the Lord's church, you cannot purchase membership in it, and you cannot "join" it. You simply obey the gospel and let God add you (Acts 2:47).

To be forgiven of sins, one must take the following steps:

---

* *Hear* the gospel (John 6:44,45; Romans 10:17).
* *Believe* it (Romans 1:16; Hebrews 11:6;John 8:24).
* *Repent* (Acts 17:30; 2 Corinthians 7:10; 2 Peter 3:9).
* *Confess* Christ (Romans 10:9,10; Acts 8:37).
* Be *baptized* (immersed) for the purpose of receiving forgiveness (Acts 2:38; 22:16; Mark 16:16; Romans 6:3,4; 1 Peter 3:21).

At baptism, one's sins are forgiven and the Lord then adds him to the church (Acts 2:38,47; 1 Corinthians 12:13).

20 Suppose a church teaches some other way for people to be saved. Would it be honoring Jesus as Lord, and would the people who believed the doctrine of that church really be saved? Answer (yes or no): _____.

If Jesus' church exists today, it must still teach just what the gospel says about salvation.

The Worship Offered in Church Assemblies

The Lord taught His church to do five things when they meet.

1. Teaching

>>>Read ACTS 2:42. <<<

21 In what activities did these disciples continue steadfastly? (a) the apostles' doctrine, (b) prayer, (c) breaking of bread, (d) all the preceding. Answer: _____.

We should teach only God's word. (Cf. Acts 20:7; 11:26; Heb. 10:25.)

2. Prayer (see Acts 2:42 above)

In Bible study, God talks to us. In prayer, we talk to God. (Cf. 1 Corinthians 14:15; Philippians 4:6; Acts 4:23-31.)

Note that Jesus is the only Mediator between God and man (1 Timothy 2:5). We should pray to God in the name of Jesus, not through saints or Mary.

3. *Giving*

>>>**Read 1 CORINTHIANS 16:1,2.** <<<

22 How did the church obtain financial income? (a) raffles and bingo, (b) bake sales and rummages, (c) collections, (d) all the preceding. Answer: _____.

23 When were the collections taken up? (a) on the seventh day of the week, (b) on the first day of the week, (c) as often as possible. Answer: _____.

24 How did the members decide how much to give? Answer: Each one gave as he had _____.

The church took up collections from the members on the first day of the week. Each member gave generously according to prosperity. The church never used tithing (requiring 10%), nor man-made fund-raising methods like bingo, raffles, rummages, etc. (Cf. 2 Cor. 8:1-5; 9:6,7.)

4. *Lord's Supper (communion or breaking of bread)*

>>> **Read 1 CORINTHIANS 11:23-26.** <<<

25&26 What do the bread and cup remind us of? Answer: The bread reminds us of Jesus' _____. The cup reminds us of Jesus' _____.

27 May we use bacon and eggs on the Lord's table? Answer (yes or no): _____.

We should eat the bread and drink the fruit of the vine in memory of Jesus' body and blood. (Cf. Matthew 26:17-30; Acts 2:42.)

>>> **Read ACTS 20:7.** <<<

28 When did the disciples break bread? (a) at Easter and Christmas, (b) on the last day of the week, (c) on the first day of the week. Answer: _____.

29 How often does the first day of the week occur? Answer (give a number): The first day of the week comes (give a number) _____ time each week.

When God specified memorial feasts, He always told people when to do them. If He said to do it on a certain day of a certain month of the year, it would be an **annual** feast (Ex. 12:6,14,24ff; Lev. 23:24,27). If He said to do it on a certain day of the month, it would be a **monthly** observance (Ezek. 46:1,6,7). If He said to do it on a certain day of the week, then it would be observed **weekly** (like the Sabbath - Ex. 20:8-11).

Likewise, God has revealed that disciples had the Lord's Supper on the first day of the week, so we should do it as often as that day occurs. The collection and communion occurred on the same day. When churches today practice annual or monthly communion, do they also take up collections only annually or monthly?

For more information about when to have the Lord's Supper, see our web site at www.gospelway.com/instruct.

5. Singing

>>> **Read EPHESIANS 5:19.** <<<

30 What act of worship is commanded here? Answer: The verse instructs us to _____ and make melody in our hearts to the Lord.

31 What purpose(s) are accomplished by singing? (a) praising God and teaching others, (b) showing off musical ability, (c) entertainment to draw big crowds, (d) all the preceding. Answer: _____.

Every New Testament passage that mentions music in worship specifies **singing** (Colossians 3:16; 1 Corinthians 14:15; Romans 15:9; Hebrews 2:12; James 5:13). There are two kinds of music - singing (vocal) and playing (instrumental).

32 Since Jesus expressly says to "**sing**," are we honoring Jesus if we add another kind of music (playing on instruments)? Answer (yes or no): _____.

To use instruments of music in worship is to follow human authority. It fails to honor Jesus just like bacon and eggs on the Lord's Table.

For more information about instrumental music in worship, see our web site at www.gospelway.com/instruct.

>>> **Read HEBREWS 10:25.** <<<

33 What error should Christians avoid? Answer: We should not forsake the _____ of ourselves together.

34 Would a church be following Jesus as Lord if it worshipped in ways that are not found in the gospel? Answer (yes or no): _____.

Jesus Is Lord

If Jesus' church exists today, it must worship by this same pattern.

The Work or Mission of the Church

>>> **Read ACTS 11:26.** <<<

35 What work did the church in Antioch accomplish? Answer: The church assembled so people could be _____.

The church is the "pillar and ground of the truth" - 1 Timothy 3:15. It teaches the gospel to the lost and edifies the members (see also Acts 11:22; 20:7; Hebrews 10:24,25; Ephesians 4:11-16; Philippians 4:14-18). The church also cares for its own physically needy members (Acts 4:32-35; 6:1-6; 1 Corinthians 16:1,2; 2 Corinthians 8 and 9; 1 Timothy 5:16).

The primary work of the church is **spiritual.** It helps people be right with God so they can receive eternal life. Jesus' church is not a social or recreational club nor a general welfare society. Any church that does these other works fails to honor the Lord. (See also John 18:36; 6:63,27; 2 Corinthians 10:3-5.)

The Organization of the Church

Universal Church Government

>>> **Read EPHESIANS 1:22,23.** <<<

36 Jesus is head over how many things to the church? Answer: Jesus is Head over _____ things to the church.

37 What is left for men to be head over in the church? (a) church laws, (b) things on earth, (c) nothing. Answer: _____.

38 Where is Jesus now (Hebrews 8:1; 1 Peter 3:22; Eph. 1:20)? Answer: Jesus is in _____.

39 Then where is the headquarters of Jesus church? (a) heaven, (b) Rome, (c) Salt Lake City. Answer: _____.

Jesus' church has no earthly headquarters or governing body. No man or group of men may make laws for the church.

Local Church Organization

>>> **Read ACTS 20:17,28 and 1 PETER 5:1-3.** <<<

40 What is the work of elders? (a) feed (shepherd) the flock, (b) oversee the church, (c) set a good example, (d) all the preceding. Answer: _____.

41 An eldership should have oversight of the work of how many churches? (a) two, (b) every one in the diocese, (c) the one among them. Answer: _____.

Note: Reading the above verses closely will show that "elder" is just another name for an overseer or "bishop" and a shepherd or "pastor."

Each local church must work to appoint a **plurality** of elders (Acts 14:23). To be appointed, these men must possess certain qualifications (1 Timothy 3:1-7; Titus 1:5-9). When they have been appointed, they guide the local church in obeying God's word. The oversight of each eldership is limited to the **one** local church where they have been appointed.

Jesus' church has no earthly headquarters or centralized institutions. Each congregation functions independently under its own officers.

>>> **Please read 1 TIMOTHY 2:11,12.** <<<

42 What must women do in spiritual teaching? (a) be in subjection, (b) not teach over men, (c) not have authority over men, (d) all the preceding. Answer: _____.

Elders (bishops) in the church must be men ("husband of one wife" – 1 Timothy 3:2). All apostles were men (Acts 1:13,21,22). Women are forbidden to lead men in the church or even to speak in congregational assemblies (1 Corinthians 14:34-37).

43 If a church changes this pattern, would it be honoring Jesus? Answer (yes or no): _____.

We have now studied the "fruits" or characteristics of Jesus' church. Since God is no respecter of persons, He still requires His church to possess these same characteristics today. Any church that does not have these characteristics, cannot be the church Jesus built.

For more information about church organization and work, please see our web site at www.gospelway.com/instruct.

Part II. How Did Modern Denominations Begin?

Jesus built one church, and the Bible tells us what it should be like. Today there are many different denominations. Is God pleased by their existence? Where did they come from?

Warnings of Departure from the Gospel

>>> Read ACTS 20:28-30. <<<

44 What danger does Paul warn about? Answer: Elders might draw away _____ after themselves.

45 Can religious leaders lead people into error? Answer (yes or no): _____.

>>> Read 2 TIMOTHY 4:2-4. <<<

46 What error will people be guilty of? Answer: They may turn from the _____ and follow fables.

>>> Read 1 TIMOTHY 4:1-3. <<<

47 What does the Spirit predict will happen? Answer: Some will _____ from the faith.

48 What particular doctrines will be taught? (a) some food (meat) should not be eaten, (b) some people should not marry, (c) both of these. Answer: _____.

Many false teachers have come among God's people. In particular, Jesus warned that error would enter among the elders, and some would forbid marriage and command to abstain from meats. God's true people must reject these false teachings. (See also Matthew 7:15-23; 15:14; Galatians 1:6-10; 1 John 4:1,6; 2 Corinthians 11:13-15; 2 John 9-11; Eph. 5:11.)

The Beginning of the Catholic Church

(Note that we do not seek to hurt people in any particular religious group. We present these facts so people can know the truth and honor Jesus as their Lord - Luke 6:46; Rev. 3:19.)

Jesus is the only head of His church. It has no man-made laws or earthly headquarters. No officers oversee more than one local church.

However, after the church began, departure occurred just as the Scriptures predicted. Certain congregations began to exalt one elder above the others. This exalted "bishop" would assume the oversight of several churches in a region called a "diocese."

Soon, bishops met in councils to issue "church laws." The first universal council, to which all churches were invited to send representatives, was in Nicea in 325 AD. Later, discussion arose regarding who would be the earthly head of the whole church. Finally, in the sixth or seventh century AD, the Bishop of Rome was generally recognized as "Pope." Clearly, this is a departure from Jesus' plan for church organization.

Meanwhile, the church was adopting other new practices. Listed below are the approximate dates when many of the practices came to be generally accepted. (Note: This historical information can be documented by checking encyclopedias or church history books.)

Practice	Date
Use of images in worship	4th century
Infant baptism	4th century
Celibacy of priests	4th century
Purgatory	6th century
Instrumental music (first used)	7th century
Confession to priest	9th century
Indulgences	12th century
Sprinkling for baptism	1311
Cup withheld from laity	1416
Infallibility of the Pope	1870

Note especially *celibacy*, which forbids priests to marry. The Catholic Church has also commanded members to abstain from meats on Fridays during Lent. This expressly fulfills 1 Timothy 4:1-3.

The changes we have described resulted in the Roman Catholic Church. Does the Catholic Church show the fruits of being Jesus' church? Contrary to its claims, the Catholic Church is not truly "the first church," but is rather the first major *apostasy* from the true church. If we wish to find Jesus' church, we must look elsewhere.

For more information about Catholicism, see our web site at www.gospelway.com/instruct.

The Beginning of Protestant Denominations

As Rome moved further from God's word, many Catholics began to object. In the 1400's and 1500's the church allowed only Latin translations of the Bible, which the common people could not understand. Then, men like John Wycliffe and William Tyndale translated the Bible into English. For this, the church burned Wycliffe's bones and made a martyr of Tyndale!

In 1517, a Catholic monk named Martin Luther nailed his "95 Theses" (or points of disagreement) to the door of a church building in Wittenburg, Germany. Other men like Zwingli and Calvin joined the movement of "protest," not to start a new church, but to "reform" the Catholic Church. Instead, however, the followers of these men eventually began new churches separate from Rome and from one another.

Here are some examples:

Name	Date	Place	Founder
Lutheran	1530	Germany	Martin Luther
Church of England	1533	England	Henry VIII
Presbyterian	1536/1560	Switzerland /Scotland	Calvin/Knox
Baptist	1609	Holland	John Smyth
Methodist	1739	England	John Wesley
Mormon	1829	America	Joseph Smith
7th Day Adventist	1846/1863	America	Miller/White
Jehovah's Witnesses	1872	America	C. Russell

(Again, this information can be verified in a good encyclopedia or church history. Note that some dates are approximate.)

Now let us compare the fruits of these denominations to the characteristics of Jesus' church.

Authority - Most denominations follow man-made creeds as law in addition to the Bible.

Origin - No Protestant denomination existed as an organized, functioning body, separate from the Catholic Church, prior to 1500 AD. They were all begun by men in times and places other the day of Pentecost in Jerusalem (Acts 2).

Name - Nearly all have names invented by men and not found in the gospel. Many names honor men and doctrines, not God and Christ.

Salvation - Most have infant baptism, sprinkling and pouring. Most teach "faith only" (baptism is not necessary to salvation).

Worship - Most have annual or monthly communion, instrumental music, holy days, tithing, and man-made fund-raising methods.

Work - Most denominations practice the "Social Gospel" - church-sponsored recreation, entertainment, etc.

Organization - Nearly all denominations have earthly headquarters, central governing bodies, boards and institutions of all kinds that centralize the work and government of the church.

Protestant leaders had some admirable goals, but all of them (or their followers) clung to basic errors of Catholicism and even added some new ones. Every Protestant denomination differs from the church of Christ on many or all of the above points. Again, if we wish to find the church belonging to Jesus, we must look elsewhere.

God's Attitude Toward Religious Division

Denominations contradict and disagree with one another. Yet people often say, "All the churches are following Jesus. It doesn't matter where you attend, or what you believe, as long as you worship the true God. Just join the church of your choice." What does Jesus say?

>>> **Read JOHN 17:20-22.** <<<

49 In what way should we be like the Father and the Son? Answer: We should be _____ as the Father and Son are.

50 In what ways do the Father and Son contradict one another? (a) about how to worship, (b) about how to be saved, (c) about what church to attend, (d) none of the preceding. (See also John 12:49,50.) Answer: _____.

The existence of denominations contradicts Jesus' prayer for unity.

>>> **Read 1 CORINTHIANS 1:10,13.** <<<

51 What does God say about division? Answer: There should be no _____ among us.

52 Is Christ divided? Does He contradict Himself? Answer (yes or no): _____.

53 Jesus does not contradict Himself, but churches do contradict one another. So are "all the churches following Jesus"? Answer (yes or no): _____.

When a preacher knowingly contradicts himself, we call him a **hypocrite**. But denominations contradict one another, yet they all say they get their teaching from Jesus. What would that make Jesus? Denominationalism violates God's law against division (Galatians 5:19-21).

>>> **Read 1 CORINTHIANS 14:33.** <<<

54 What is God's relationship to confusion? Answer: God is not the author (cause) of _____.

55 Is the existence of many churches confusing? Answer (yes or no): _____.

56 Is God the source of all the denominations? Answer (yes or no) _____.

God did not create the modern denominations, so they must have been begun by **men**. They are not in the Bible, therefore they exist contrary to God's authority. When churches disagree, one may be right and the others wrong, or they may all be wrong, but they cannot all be right!

>>> **Read EPHESIANS 4:3-6.** <<<

We must strive to keep the unity of the Spirit in the bond of peace.

57 How many true "God and Fathers" are there? Answer (give a number): There is _____ God and Father.

58 Can we please God if we think there are many acceptable gods, and we may just worship the god of our choice? Answer (yes or no): _____.

59&60 How many "bodies" and "faiths" are there? Answer (give a number): There is _____ body and _____ faith.

61 Can we please God if we think there are hundreds of acceptable bodies and faiths, so we can just take our choice? Answer (yes or no): _____.

There may be many **false** gods, but there is only **one true** God. In the same way, there is only one true **body** (church) and only one true **faith**. All others are **false**. [Cf. 1 Corinthians 12:12-20.]

>>> **Read 2 CORINTHIANS 6:17-7:1.** <<<

61 To be God's true children, what must we do about practices and churches that God has not authorized? Answer: We must come out from among them and be

_____.

The Lord established **one** church, not many denominations. He condemned division. He requires us to follow His true gospel pattern, but Catholic and Protestant churches are departures from His pattern. Therefore, we must not be members of any of these groups. Are you a member of a man-made church? [Cf. 2 John 9-11; Eph. 5:11; Matt. 15:14]

For more information about denominationalism and modern religious confusion and division, see our web site at www.gospelway.com/instruct.

The Existence of Jesus' True Church Today

If neither the Catholic nor the Protestant churches are Jesus' church, where can we find it? Does it exist? Since we must be members of His church to be saved, how can people today be saved?

>>> **Read 1 PETER 1:22-25.** <<<

63 How do we purify our souls? Answer: We purify our souls in obeying the _____.

64 What is the seed by which we are born again? Answer: We are born again by God's _____.

65 How long will this seed endure? Answer:

_____.

"The seed is the word of God" - Luke 8:11. God's creations, including the church, reproduce by means of seed. When men hear the gospel with receptive hearts, they will believe and obey. As a result, they are "born again" into God's family, the church. (See James 1:18; Luke 8:15; Romans 1:16; 10:17; Mark 16:15,16; John 3:3-5.)

>>> **Read GALATIANS 6:7.** <<<

66 How does the seed relate to the harvest? Answer: Whatever a man sows, that is what he will

_____.

At any time or place, the same seed always produces the same kind of living thing. Like seed, doctrines reproduce after their own kind. To get the right "fruit," we must plant the right "seed." Denominations do not produce the right *fruit,* because they plant the wrong **seed**.

67 Suppose you believed and obeyed Buddhist doctrine. What would that make you? (a) a Christian, (b) a Hindu, (c) a Buddhist. Answer: _____.

Man-made doctrines reproduce after their own kind and make people members of man-made religious groups.

68 In the first century, when people obeyed Jesus' gospel, what kind of Christians did they become and what church did they become members of? (a) Lutherans, (b) Catholics, (c) just Christians, members of Jesus' church. Answer: _____.

69 If you were to obey simply the gospel today, without any man-made changes, what kind of Christian would you become and what church would that make you a member of? (a) the same as in the first century, (b) a modern denomination, (c) no one knows. Answer: _____.

Anytime and anyplace, when a person obeys only the gospel, he becomes a **Christian**, exactly like people were in the first century. They were not members of any of the modern denominations and neither should people today be. The Lord will add people today to **His** church, just as He did in the first century (Acts 2:47). These saved people must then work and worship with a faithful local church.

Conclusion

People who wish to be saved must be members of the Lord's one true church. Since salvation is free to all, **you too** can obey the gospel and enter Jesus' true church (Matthew 28:18-20; Romans 1:16; Acts 2:39; Titus 2:11,12; 2 Peter 3:9). Have you obeyed Jesus? Are you part of His one true church? If not, why not obey Him today?

Personal application questions:

What church have you been a member of in the past? _____

Does that church properly teach people how to be saved from sin as taught in the gospel? _____

Does that church teach the gospel truth about how to worship God, what the church should be called, etc.? _____

What conclusions do you reach regarding what the Bible teaches about the existence of Catholic and Protestant denominations? _____

How can a person be faithful to the Lord today in an age with so much religious error and confusion? _____
_____

If you have been part of a church, is that church following Jesus' true pattern for His church, or is it a group that has departed from His way? _____

While you have been studying this course, have you made any significant changes in your faith, spiritual conduct, church membership, or relationship with God? If so, please explain.
_____

Answers to the Questions

Note that we have attempted to list correct answers, but these answers may be worded in other ways, especially when students use other translations. Any answers that mean the same would likewise be correct, but we cannot list all possible variations here.

Why Should You Believe in God, Jesus, and the Bible?

1 To please God, what must we believe? (a) whatever our parents taught us, (b) whatever our preacher says, (c) that God exists and rewards those who diligently seek Him. Answer: c.

2 Where did the Scriptures come from? (a) they are inspired by God, (b) they express the opinions of men, (c) they are ancient legends of unknown origin. Answer: a.

3&4 What did Thomas call Jesus? Answer: My **Lord** and my **God**.

5&6 What must we believe in order to have eternal life? Answer: Jesus is the **Christ**, the Son of **God (the living God)**.

7 God did not leave Himself without what? (a) people, (b) witness, (c) time, (d) money. Answer: b.

8 What does this verse say is the origin of life? (a) life on earth has always existed, (b) an unplanned accident of nature produced the first primitive life by spontaneous generation in an ancient swamp, (c) life on earth was created by a living, wise, powerful God. Answer: c.

9 What kind of offspring do living things have? (a) the same kind as the parents, (b) with enough time, entirely different things may evolve, (c) you never know. Answer: a.

10 Man is created in whose image? Answer: In the image of **God**.

11 Man has dominion over what? (a) fish, (b) birds, (c) animals, (d) earth, (e) all the preceding. Answer: e.

12 How can we see the power and Deity (Godhead) of God? Answer: We see them by the things God **made (created)**.

13 What do the heavens declare? Answer: The heavens declare the **glory** (majesty, greatness) of God.

14 As a house must have a maker, who ultimately built all things? Answer: The ultimate maker of all things is **God**.

15 Every effect must have an adequate what? Answer: **cause (source, origin)**.

16 Uriah was of what nationality? Answer: Uriah was a **Hittite**.

17&18 Name the two cities the Israelites built in Egypt. Answer: They built **Pithom** and **Raamses (Rameses)**.

19 What is the shape of the earth? (a) circle, (b) flat, (c) cylinder. Answer: a.

20 How is the earth held up? Answer: The earth hangs on **nothing**.

21 Fish pass through what in the seas? Answer: They swim or pass through the **paths (lanes)** of the seas.

22 What does this verse tell us about rivers? (a) rivers run to the sea, (b) the sea does not get fuller, (c) rivers go back where they were before, (d) all the preceding. Answer: d.

23 Consider religious teachers who write by **human** wisdom. How often do you find them completely agreeing among themselves? (a) they always agree on everything, (b) they usually agree, (c) complete agreement is rare. Answer: c.

24 If the 40 Bible writers, having such different backgrounds, do agree completely, what would this indicate? (a) they were not writing by their own wisdom, (b) the Bible must be the product of one supreme Mind, (c) God exists, (d) the Bible is God's word, (e) all the preceding. Answer: e.

25 Can men consistently predict the future? (yes or no) Answer: no.

26 What can God do that false gods cannot do? Answer: God can predict the **future** (things to come).

27 God refused to allow His praise to be given to whom? Answer: **idols** (graven images, carved images).

28 If a man tries to predict the future and fails, what can we know? Answer: We can know that what he speaks is not from **God (the Lord)**.

29 What did Jesus say about Old Testament Scriptures? (a) they no longer have any value, (b) He was unable to understand them, (c) they spoke about Him and He fulfilled them, (d) all the preceding. Answer: c.

Jesus Is Lord

30 The miracle was: Jesus raised a man from the **dead (grave, tomb)**.

31&32 The miracle was: Jesus **walked** on the **water** (sea, lake).

33 The miracle was: Jesus fed (give a number) **5000 (five thousand, 5,000)** men with five loaves and two fish.

34 What did Jesus say His works proved? (a) that the Father sent Him, (b) that He was a skilled magician, (c) that God will do miracles today for anyone who loves Him. Answer: a.

35 What purpose was served by the miracles done through Paul? (a) they made Paul wealthy, (b) they proved the Lord spoke through Paul, (c) they proved everybody can do miracles, (d) all the preceding. Answer: b.

36 What did the rulers say Peter and John had done? Answer: They had done a great **miracle (sign, wonder)**.

37 What did the rulers say Jesus did? Answer: They said He did many **signs (wonders, miracles)**.

38&39 The resurrection declared Jesus to be who? Answer: He was declared to be the **Son** of **God (the Father)** by the resurrection from the dead.

40,41,&42 List in historical order three facts Paul preached about Jesus in verses 3,4. Answers: Jesus **died**, He was **buried**, and He **arose (rose again, was raised)** on the third day.

43 Verses 5-8 list how many times that Jesus appeared to people after His resurrection? Answer: (give a number) **six (6)** times. (Note: The six times are: Cephas, the 12, 500 brethren, James, all the apostles, and Paul.)

Is Jesus Really Your Lord?

1 How many people commit sin? Answer: **All (everyone)** have sinned.

2 What is the consequence of sin? Answer: The wages of sin is **death**.

3 Through whom can we receive eternal life? (a) Mohammed, (b) Jesus, (c) our parents, (d) no one. Answer: b.

4 What did Jesus do to save us? Answer: He **died** (gave His life, was crucified) for us.

5 What characteristic of God does this demonstrate? Answer: It demonstrates God's **love** for us.

6 When Jesus died, was He dying for **you**? Answer ("Yes" or "no"): **yes**.

7 When Jesus suffered, whose sins was He suffering for? (a) His own sins, (b) sins of other people, including you and me. Answer: b.

8 How did Thomas know Jesus had been raised? (a) he saw and touched Him, (b) he just heard about it, (c) he dreamed about it. Answer: a.

9&10 Whom did Thomas confess Jesus to be? Answer: My **Lord** and my **God**.

11 How can we believe Jesus is Lord and God even though we have not seen Him? (a) by guessing, (b) by examining the evidence in the Bible, (c) by taking a preacher's word for it. Answer: b.

12 What blessing can we have if we believe? Answer: We can have **life (eternal life)** in His name.

13 How many people will be judged? Answer: We must **all (everyone)** appear before the judgment seat.

14 Who will judge us? (a) our priest, (b) Buddha, (c) Jesus. Answer: c.

15 On what basis will Jesus decide our reward? (a) what our parents did, (b) what Adam did, (c) what we did, (d) all the preceding. Answer: c.

16 What final destinies face us? (a) either eternal life or eternal destruction, (b) all go to heaven, (c) death is the end of our existence. Answer: a.

17 How many follow the broad road? Answer: **Many** enter the broad way.

18 How many follow the narrow way? Answer: **Few** find the narrow way.

19 What must we do to enter the kingdom of heaven? (a) just have faith, (b) call Jesus "Lord," (c) do God's will, (d) just be religious. Answer: c.

20 To be Jesus' disciple, what must we do? (a) just believe in Him, (b) just learn His will, (c) learn His will and obey it (abide in it)? Answer: c.

21 If we know and abide in Jesus' word, what will it do for us? Answer: Make us **free** from sin (see v34).

22 Do we respect our Lord if we do not obey Him? Answer: (Yes or no): **no**.

23 If we have been practicing some activity that is nowhere taught in the Scriptures, what should we do? (a) quit serving God, (b) find a preacher who justifies the practice, (c) quit participating in it. Answer: c.

24 What is the goal of a disciple or servant? Answer: The disciple's goal is to be like his **teacher (master, lord, ruler, instructor)**.

25&26 What did Jesus leave for us? Answer: Jesus left an **example (pattern)** so we should follow in His **steps**.

27 How did Jesus live? Answer: Jesus lived without committing **sin (evil, wickedness)** .

28 What must a person be willing to give up to be Jesus' disciple (a) loved ones, (b) possessions, (c) his life, (d) all the preceding. Answer: d.

29 How many spiritual masters (lords) can a person serve? Answer: You can have only **one (1)** Master.

30&31 What should be our greatest concern in life? Answer: Seek first the **kingdom** of God and His **righteousness**.

32&33 If disciples don't bear fruit and abide in Christ (v2,4-6), what happens to them? Answer: They are picked up and thrown into the **fire** (flame) and are **burned (burned up, consumed)**.

34 Though Paul was an apostle who had preached to others, what concern did he have? (a) he might be disqualified or rejected, (b) some babies might not be baptized, (c) he might be among the elect. Answer: a.

35 One who thinks he stands must take heed for what (10:12)? Answer: Take heed lest he **fall**.

36 We too must guard against what? (a) an evil heart of unbelief, (b) departing from God, (c) being hardened through the deceitfulness of sin, (d) all the preceding. Answer: d.

37 To partake with Christ, what must we do? Answer: We must hold our confidence (faith) steadfast to the **end**.

38 Can a person please God and be saved eternally if he does not have faith (Hebrews 11:6; Revelation 21:8)? Answer: ("Yes" or "no.") **no**.

39 What was Simon's condition after he sinned again (see vv. 20-23)? (a) his heart was not right, (b) he was guilty of wickedness, (c) he was in the gall of bitterness and the bond of iniquity, (d) he would perish if he did not repent and pray, (e) all the preceding. Answer: e.

40 What would be their condition if they went back to the Old Testament practice of binding circumcision? (a) Christ would profit them nothing, (b) they would be severed from Christ, (c) they would be fallen from grace, (d) all the preceding. Answer: d.

How Can We Learn Jesus' Will?

1&2 What did Jesus say the Spirit of truth would do for the apostles? Answer: The Spirit would **guide** them into **all** truth.

3 How can people believe in Jesus even when they have not seen Him? (a) they can't believe, (b) they need a modern-day prophet, (c) they can believe by reading what the inspired men wrote in the Bible. Answer: c.

4 What blessing can people receive if they believe what is written? Answer: By believing we can have **life (eternal life, everlasting life)** in His name.

5 What did Paul do with the knowledge revealed to him? (a) he wrote it down, (b) he kept it a secret, (c) it is still an unknown mystery. Answer: a

6 How can other people learn what Paul knew? Answer: We can understand when we **read** what he wrote.

7 Whose commands did Paul write? Answer: Paul wrote the commands of the **Lord** (God, Jesus, Christ).

8 How much of God's will did Paul teach to others? (a) he kept back parts that were needed, (b) he preached the whole counsel of God, (c) there were important truths that he never even received. Answer: b

9 How much of God's will had people in Peter's lifetime received? Answer: They received **all** things pertaining to life and godliness.

10 For what purposes are the Scriptures profitable? (a) teaching and instructing us in righteousness, (b) reproving and correcting us, (c) completely providing all good works, (d) all the preceding. Answer: d

11 If the Scriptures provide us to all good works, then do we need some standard of religious authority in addition to the Bible? (yes or no) Answer: **no.**

12 What did Jesus expect his hearers to do? Answer: They were supposed to hear and **understand**.

13 How did these people determine whether or not the things they heard were true? (a) they searched the Scriptures daily, (b) they needed a college education, (c) they needed a priest to explain it to them. Answer: a

14 God is not the author of what? Answer: **confusion** (disorder).

15 Peter was writing so that people would have a record of his teachings after he died. What would this message do for them? Answer: It would **remind (put them in mind)** them of the apostles' commands.

16 By what standard will men be judged? (a) by their own consciences, (b) by the teachings of their priests, (c) by Jesus' words. Answer: c

17 What is the seed by which we are born again? Answer: We are born again by the incorruptible seed, which is the **word (gospel)** of God.

18 How long will God's word endure? (a) forever, (b) 2 generations, (c) like a plant that grows then dies, it was lost in the middle ages. Answer: a

19 How long will the truth be with us? Answer: The truth will be with us *forever (always)*.

20 When is a woman free from her husband? (a) when she divorces him, (b) when she becomes a Christian, (c) when he dies. Answer: c

21 What is our relation to the law? (a) we are subject to it, (b) we are freed from it and joined to Christ, (c) we should still keep parts of it. Answer: b

22&23 What did Jesus do to these two covenants? Answer: He **took away (removed, set aside, taketh away)** the first and **established** (instituted, inaugurated) the second.

24&25 What did Christ do to the handwriting of ordinances? Answer: He took it **away (out of the way, aside)** nailing it to His **cross**.

26 Should we let people judge us for not keeping the sabbath? (yes or no) Answer: **no**

27 How does Jesus describe our worship if it is based on human doctrine (v9) ? (a) it is vain, (b) it is acceptable, (c) it doesn't matter. Answer: a

28 What is the condition of one who preaches a different gospel? Answer: He is **accursed (anathema, eternally condemned).**

29 What happens to someone who teaches things not found in the teachings that come from Jesus? Answer: He does not have **God** (the Father, the Son).

30 If our family is involved in practices not found in the gospel, should we still practice as they do? (yes or no) Answer: **no**

31 Even before his conversion, Paul was sincere and had a good conscience. At that time was he (a) right, (b) wrong, (c) it didn't matter? Answer: b

32 Should we accept what our preacher says if he cannot show it in the Bible? (yes or no) Answer: **no**

How Can You Be Sure Jesus Has Forgiven Your Sins?

1 What is sin? Sin is: (a) breaking social customs, (b) displeasing other people, (c) violating human tradition, (d) transgression or breaking of God's law (lawlessness). Answer: d.

2 Sin is something a person: (a) commits (practices), (b) inherits. Answer: a.

3 How do people become slaves of sin? (a) they inherit a corrupt nature from Adam, (b) everyone is born a slave of sin, (c) whoever commits sin (presents himself to obey sin) is a slave of sin. Answer: c.

4 What sins was Jesus guilty of? (a) He was born a sinner, (b) He was guilty of Adam's sin, (c) He was guilty of no sins because He committed no sins. Answer: c.

5 Who bears the guilt of a person's sins? Answer: The wickedness of the wicked will be upon (charged against) **himself (the wicked person, the sinner).**

6 What sins are we guilty of? (a) just the ones we commit, (b) our father's, (c) Adam's. Answer: a.

7 Who will enter the kingdom of heaven (v21)? Answer: He who **does (doeth, obeys, keeps)** the will of the Father.

8 Jesus will reject those who work (practice/do) what (v23)? Answer: **iniquity (lawlessness, sin, evil, wickedness)**

*9 To receive eternal life, what must we do (v7,10)? Answer: We must continue in **doing good (well doing, doing right)**.

10&11 Who will receive tribulation and anguish (v8,9)? Answer: Those who reject (do not obey) the **truth** but obey (follow) **unrighteousness (evil, wickedness)**.

12 How many people must appear before Jesus' judgment seat? Answer: **all (everyone, each one)**.

13 On what basis will each one be judged? (a) what his parents did, (b) what he has done in the body, (c) what Adam did. Answer: b.

14 When people sacrificed their babies to idols, what kind of blood did they shed? Answer: They shed **innocent (guiltless)** blood.

15 God is the Father of what? Answer: Our **spirits (souls)**.

16 What is taught about little children? (a) they inherit the sin of Adam, (b) we must be converted and become like little children to enter the kingdom of God, (c) they are sinners. Answer: b.

17 What did Peter tell the people to believe (v36)? (a) Jesus is Lord and Christ, (b) people can save themselves without Jesus, (c) it does not matter what we believe if we are sincere, (d) all the preceding. Answer: a.

18&19 What did Peter command them to do (v38)? Answer: **Repent** and be **baptized**.

20 For what purpose were they to do this (v38)? Answer: For the **remission (forgiveness, cleansing, loosing)** of sins.

21 As Philip taught about Jesus, what did the eunuch want (v36)? (a) baptism, (b) money, (c) a direct revelation from the Holy Spirit. Answer: a.

22 What did the eunuch have to do first (v37)? (a) pray for forgiveness, (b) tell Philip that he believed in Jesus, (c) pay a fee. Answer: b.

23 What did the Lord tell Saul to do (v6)? (a) wait in the city to be told what he must do, (b) pray through at the mourner's bench, (c) send a financial contribution. Answer: a.

24&25 What did Ananias tell him he must do (22:16)? Answer: He said to be **baptized** and wash away his **sins**.

26 What must one do to come to Jesus? (a) see a vision, (b) learn the word of God, (c) pray for a direct message from the Spirit. Answer: b.

27 Can one be saved without hearing the gospel? (yes or no) Answer: **no**.

28 What is the power of God to salvation? (a) human wisdom, (b) the gospel, (c) man-made creeds. Answer: b.

29 Who can be saved by the gospel? (a) all who truly believe, (b) anyone who has a good conscience, (c) anyone who is sincere. Answer: a.

30 What does God command men to do? Answer: **repent**.

31 How many people must do this? (a) some, (b) all, (c) none. Answer: b.

32 What is repentance (note Matthew 21:28,29)? (a) never committing sin, (b) not getting caught, (c) changing our minds about our sins. Answer: c.

33 Besides believing, what else must we do to be saved? (a) confess Jesus, (b) believe what our parents did, (c) obey the 10 commands. Answer: a.

What Does Jesus Teach about Obedience and Baptism?

1 Who is acceptable to God? (a) one who just fears him, (b) one who calls Jesus "Lord," (c) one who fears Him and works righteousness. Answer: **c**.

2 Jesus is author (source) of salvation to whom? Answer: To all who **obey** Him.

3 To be set free from sin, what must people do? Answer: They must **obey** from the heart the doctrine delivered.

4 We purify our souls in doing what? (a) in simply believing in Jesus, (b) in obeying the truth, (c) in praying for forgiveness. Answer: **b**.

5 If we love Him, what will we do? Answer: We will keep (obey) His **commands** (commandments).

6 What avails in Christ? Answer: What avails is faith **working (expressing itself, operating)** through love.

7 What is the condition of faith without works (v17,20,26)? (a) it is dead (barren), (b) it saves us, (c) it is like the faith of Abraham. Answer: **a**.

8 We are justified by works and not by what (v24)? Answer: We are not justified by **faith only (faith alone)**.

9 One who has repented should do what? (a) live like before, (b) teach that works do not matter, (c) do works worthy of repentance. Answer: **c**.

10 Which of the following must one give up? (a) stealing, (b) homosexuality, (c) drunkenness, (d) an adulterous remarriage, (e) all the preceding. (See also 1 Cor. 6:9-11; Gal. 5:19-21; Matt. 19:9; Luke 3:8-14.) Answer: **e**.

11 God will reward each one according to what (v6)? Answer: According to his **deeds (works, what he has done)**.

12 Eternal life will be given to whom (v7,10)? (a) those who continue patiently in well-doing and who work good, (b) those who just believe, (c) those who have godly relatives. Answer: **a**.

13 Tribulation and anguish will be given to whom (8,9)? Answer: Those who **do not obey (disobey, reject)** the truth but work (do) evil.

14 Flaming fire and everlasting destruction await whom? (a) those who know not God, (b) those who obey not the gospel, (c) both of these. Answer: **c**.

15 How many true Heavenly Fathers are there? Answer (give a number): **one (1)**.

16 How many true baptisms are there? Answer (give a number): **one (1)** .

17 When were Saul's sins washed away? (a) on the road to Damascus, (b) before he was baptized, (c) as a result of his baptism? Answer: **c**.

18 Note that Saul had previously believed in Jesus and had been praying (9:1-6,11). Most churches would say he was already saved before baptism. But was he? Answer (Yes or No): **no**.

19 Into what are we baptized? (a) Jesus and His death, (b) a particular denomination, (c) a social club. Answer: **a**.

20 According to what we have earlier learned, can a person be saved outside Jesus and without His blood? Answer (Yes or No): **no**.

21 For each person there must be a point at which he first receives forgiveness. He is in sin before that point, but afterwards, he is forgiven. At what point does this occur? (a) the moment we believe, (b) when we pray for forgiveness, (c) when we are baptized. (See also Galatians 3:27.) Answer: **c**.

22 When does remission of sins come? (a) before one repents and is baptized, (b) as a result of repenting and being baptized. Answer: **b**.

23 Can one be saved without repentance? Answer (Yes or No): **no**.

24 Can one be saved without baptism? Answer (Yes or No): **no**.

25 What must one do to be saved? Answer: He who believes and is **baptized** will be saved.

26 When is one saved? (a) before baptism, (b) as a result of baptism. Answer: **b**.

27 How is baptism described? (a) sprinkling, (b) pouring, (c) burial and resurrection, (d) all the preceding. Answer: **c**.

28 How is the eunuch's baptism described? (a) he was sprinkled, (b) water was poured on him, (c) he went down into the water and came up out of it. Answer: **c**.

29 When denominations sprinkle or pour, does the person "go down into" the water and "come up out of it"? Answer (Yes or No): **no**.

30 Before one can be baptized, he must understand the gospel (John 6:44,45), believe (Mark 16:15,16; Acts 8:12), repent (Acts 2:38), and confess (Romans 10:9,10). Can babies do all these things? Answer (Yes or No): **no**.

31 Baptized people are members of the church and must participate in its work and worship (1 Corinthians 12:13,25,26;

10:16,17; 11:23-29; Ephesians 4:16). Can babies do these things? Answer (Yes or No): **no**.

Where Can You Find the Church that Belongs to Jesus?

1 How did Jesus make the church His? Answer: He purchased the church with His **blood**.

2 Can we be saved without Jesus' blood? (yes or no) Answer: **no**

3 Then can we be saved outside Jesus' church? (yes or no) Answer: **no**

4 For whom is Christ the Savior? (a) the nation of Israel only, (b) the body (church), (c) all people will be saved. Answer: b

5 How can false teachers be identified? (a) by their outward appearance, (b) by their unkind manners, (c) by their fruits. Answer: c

6 What are the "fruits" of God's followers? (a) they do the will of the Father, (b) they just call Jesus "Lord," (c) they just believe. Answer: a

7 Who is Head over all things to the church? (a) John the Baptist, (b) Peter, (c) Jesus, (d) Mohammed, (e) a human headquarters. Answer: c

8 Whose control, then, should the church submit to? Answer: The control of **Jesus (Christ)**.

9 What must be done in Jesus' name (by His authority)? Answer: **Whatever (whatsoever, everything)** we do.

10 What happens if we do not abide in the teachings of Jesus? Answer: We do not have **God (the Father, the Son)**.

11 What does God think of worship that is based on man-made teachings? (a) it is vain, (b) He encourages it, (c) it doesn't matter. Answer: a

12 What happens if we preach a different gospel? Answer: We are **accursed (anathema, eternally condemned)**.

13 Would a church be honoring Jesus as Lord if it follows doctrines or practices not found in the Bible? (yes or no) Answer: **no**

14 What did Jesus promise to build? (a) a social club, (b) an entertainment, recreational club, (c) His church, (d) all the preceding. Answer: c

15 Did the church exist when Jesus said this? (yes or no) Answer: **no**

16 How many churches did Jesus promise to build? (a) one, (b) ten, (c) hundreds. Answer: a

17 Who was adding people to His body (the church)? (Cf. v38,41.) Answer: The **Lord (Jesus, Christ)**.

18 Suppose men begin a church at a place and time other than Jerusalem on Pentecost. Would it be Jesus' church? (yes or no) Answer: **no**.

19 What sin occurred at Corinth? (a) groups were named after men, (b) men were exalted instead of Jesus, (c) division, (d) all the preceding. Answer: d

20 Suppose a church teaches some other way for people to be saved. Would it be honoring Jesus as Lord, and would the people who believed the doctrine of that church really be saved? (yes or no) Answer: **no**.

21 In what activities did these disciples continue steadfastly? (a) the apostles' doctrine, (b) prayer, (c) breaking of bread, (d) all the preceding. Answer: d

22 How did the church obtain financial income? (a) raffles & bingo, (b) bake-sales & rummages, (c) collections, (d) all the preceding. Answer: c

23 When were the collections taken up? (a) on the seventh day of the week, (b) on the first day of the week, (c) as often as possible. Answer: b

24 How did the members decide how much to give? Answer: Each one gave according as he had **prospered (received, income)**.

25&26 What do the bread and cup remind us of? Answer: The bread reminds us of Jesus' **body (flesh, death)** and the cup reminds us of Jesus' **blood**.

27 May we use bacon and eggs on the Lord's table? (yes or no) Answer: **no**

28 When did the disciples break bread? (a) at Easter and Christmas, (b) on the last day of the week, (c) on the first day of the week. Answer: c

29 How often does the first day of the week occur? Answer: The first day of the week comes (give a number) **one (1)** time each week.

30 What act of worship is commanded here? Answer: The verse instructs us to **sing** and make melody in our hearts to the Lord.

31 What purpose(s) are accomplished by singing? (a) praising God and teaching others, (b) showing off musical ability, (c) entertainment to draw big crowds, (d) all the preceding. Answer: a.

32 Since Jesus expressly says to "**sing**," are we honoring Jesus if we add another kind of music (playing on instruments)? (yes or no) Answer: **no**

33 What error should Christians avoid? Answer: We should not forsake the **assembling (gathering, meeting)** of ourselves together.

34 Would a church be following Jesus as Lord if it worshipped in ways that are not found in the gospel? (yes or no) Answer: **no**

35 What work did the church in Antioch accomplish? Answer: The church assembled so people could be **taught (instructed)**.

36 Jesus is head over how many things to the church? Answer: Jesus is Head over **all** things to the church.

37 What is left for men to be head over in the church? (a) church laws, (b) things on earth, (c) nothing. Answer: c

38 Where is Jesus now (Hebrews 8:1; 1 Peter 3:22; Eph. 1:20)? Answer: Jesus is in **heaven (heavenly places, heavenly realms, God's right hand)**.

39 Then where is the headquarters of Jesus church? (a) heaven, (b) Rome, (c) Salt Lake City. Answer: a.

40 What is the work of elders? (a) feed (shepherd) the flock, (b) oversee the church, (c) set a good example, (d) all the preceding. Answer: d

41 An eldership should have oversight of the work of how many churches? (a) two, (b) every one in the diocese, (c) the one among them. Answer: c

42 What must women do in spiritual teaching? (a) be in subjection, (b) not teach over men, (c) not have authority over men, (d) all the preceding.

43 If a church changes this pattern, would it be honoring Jesus? Answer (yes or no): **no**.

44 What danger does Paul warn about? Answer: Elders might draw away **disciples (followers)** after themselves.

45 Can religious leaders lead people into error? (yes or no) Answer: **yes**

46 What error will people be guilty of? Answer: They may turn from the **truth (sound doctrine, gospel)** and follow fables.

47 What does the Spirit predict will happen? Answer: Some will **depart (abandon, leave, fall away)** from the faith.

48 What particular doctrines will be taught? (a) some food (meat) should not be eaten, (b) some people should not marry, (c) both of these. Answer: c.

49 In what way should we be like the Father and the Son? Answer: We should be **one** (united) as the Father and Son are.

50 In what ways do the Father and Son contradict one another? (a) about how to worship, (b) about how to be saved, (c) about what church to attend, (d) none of the preceding. (See also John 12:49,50.) Answer: d

51 What does God say about division? Answer: There should be no **divisions (schisms)** among us.

52 Is Christ divided? Does He contradict Himself? (yes or no) Answer: **no**.

53 Jesus does not contradict Himself, but churches do contradict one another. So are "all the churches following Jesus"? (yes or no) Answer: **no**.

54 What is God's relationship to confusion? Answer: God is not the author of **confusion (disorder, disunity)**.

55 Is the existence of many churches confusing? (yes or no) Answer: **yes**

56 Is God the source of all the denominations? (yes or no) Answer: **no**

57 How many true "God and Fathers" are there? Answer: There is **one (1)** God and Father.

58 Can we please God if we think there are many acceptable gods, and we may just worship the god of our choice? (yes or no) Answer: **no**

59&60 How many "bodies" and "faiths" are there? Answer: There is **one (1)** body and **one (1)** faith.

61 Can we please God if we think there are hundreds of acceptable bodies and faiths, so we can just take our choice? (yes or no) Answer: **no**

62 To be God's true children, what must we do about practices and churches that God has not authorized? Answer: We must come out from among them and be **separate**.

63 How do we purify our souls? Answer: We purify our souls in obeying the **truth (word of God, gospel)**.

64 What is the seed by which we are born again? Answer: We are born again by God's **word** (gospel, truth).

65 How long will this seed endure? Answer: **forever**.

66 How does the seed relate to the harvest? Answer: Whatever a man sows, that is what he will **reap (harvest)**.

67 Suppose you believed and obeyed Buddhist doctrine. What would that make you? (a) a Christian, (b) a Hindu, (c) a Buddhist. Answer: c

68 In the first century, when people obeyed Jesus' gospel, what kind of Christians did they become and what church did they become members of? (a) Lutherans, (b) Catholics, (c) just Christians, members of Jesus' church. Answer: c

69 If you were to obey simply the gospel today, without any man-made changes, what kind of Christian would you become and what church would that make you a member of? (a) the same as in the first century, (b) a modern denomination, (c) no one knows. Answer: a

Jesus Is Lord

Printed books, booklets, and tracts available at
www.lighttomypath.net/sales
Free Bible study articles online at
www.gospelway.com/instruct
Free Bible courses online at
www.biblestudylessons.com
Free class books at
www.biblestudylessons.com/classbooks
Free commentaries on Bible books at
www.gospelway.com/instruct/commentary
Contact the author at
www.gospelway.com/instruct/comments
Free e-mail Bible study newsletter -
www.gospelway.com/instruct/update_subscribe.htm

24127162R00052

Made in the USA
Middletown, DE
15 September 2015